LOCAL GOVERNMENT G

Financial and Legal Aspects of
Implementing the Local Government Act 2000

LOCAL GOVERNMENT GOVERNANCE

Financial and Legal Aspects of
Implementing the Local Government Act 2000

General Editors

Richard Lester, formerly First Vice-President, ACSeS and currently Consultant, Eversheds
Sandra Moss, Barrister, Manager of the CIPFA Better Governance and Counter-Fraud Forum

Contributors

Division 1 – Modernising Democracy
Claer Lloyd-Jones (with a team from Brighton & Hove City Council), Vice-President ACSeS and City Solicitor and Head of Corporate Governance at Brighton & Hove City Council

Division II – Ethical Standards
Mark Heath, Head of Legal Services, Southampton City Council

Division III – Community Focus
Graeme Creer, City Solicitor, Liverpool City Council

Division IV – Financial Property
Michael Crich, Consultant

Division V – Employment Implications
Tim Rothwell, Managing Director, GWT Rothwell

Butterworths
London, Dublin and Edinburgh

United Kingdom	Butterworths, a Division of Reed Elsevier (UK) Ltd, Halsbury House, 35 Chancery Lane, LONDON WC2A 1EL and 4 Hill Street, EDINBURGH EH2 3JZ
Australia	Butterworths, a Division of Reed International Books Australia Pty Ltd, CHATSWOOD, New South Wales
Canada	Butterworths Canada Ltd, MARKHAM, Ontario
Hong Kong	Butterworths Asia (Hong Kong), HONG KONG
India	Butterworths India, NEW DELHI
Ireland	Butterworths (Ireland) Ltd, DUBLIN
Malaysia	Malayan Law Journal Sdn Bhd, KUALA LUMPUR
New Zealand	Butterworths of New Zealand Ltd, WELLINGTON
Singapore	Butterworths Asia, SINGAPORE
South Africa	Butterworths Publishers (Pty) Ltd, DURBAN
USA	Lexis Law Publishing, CHARLOTTESVILLE, Virginia

A CIP Catalogue record for this book is available from the British Library.

ISBN 0-406-94153-X

9 780406 941534

Typeset by Kerrypress Ltd, Luton, Beds
Printed and bound by Bookcraft (Bath) Ltd, Midsomer Norton, Avon

FOREWORD

Up and down the country local authorities are grappling with the great challenge of our time, 'modernisation'.

It is not by any means an easy challenge. There are so many different (though interconnected) elements to a modernisation programme that advocates such high standards. Alongside the restructuring of local authorities, the Local Government Act 2000 has promoted the importance of scrutiny, accountability and ethics.

In view of this, local authority lawyers, accountants and managers generally are helping authorities to make significant progress, to be more innovative, flexible, responsible and accountable. They are working towards the implementation of codes of conduct, new powers and monitoring whilst ensuring that governance sits comfortably with Best Value, finance and employment issues.

'Change' and 'risk' are opposite sides of the same coin. Authoritative guidance, both internally from management teams and externally from the sharing of experience and advice, is crucial to achieve the balance between change and risk. Through ambitious and skillful management the ideals of modernising democracy, ethical standards, community focus and financial property can be achieved.

Local Government Governance is designed to assist those managing the implementation of such changes with practical advice and guidance in order to transform ideals into reality.

Chris Hurford
President – CIPFA

PREFACE

The term 'governance' is one which has gained increasing prominence in the language of local government in recent times. It is defined in the dictionary as 'the act or manner of governing'.

The Local Government Act 2000 and its implementation bring governance to the fore. For those of us working at the corporate centre of local government the concept of good governance has risen very much up our agendas as we advise our councils of all the implications of the 2000 Act.

In drafting new constitutions and putting into place all the arrangements necessary to implement those constitutions, in whatever form, we are to a significant extent re-inventing the governing of our local authorities. The Act has provided us with both an unprecedented opportunity and a challenge to help shape the way our councils are going to be governed in the twenty-first century. These are exciting as well as demanding times for lawyers and administrators in local government.

Given that background, the publication of *Local Government Governance* could not be better timed. The approach adopted is an extremely practical one that covers all aspects of the governance agenda. Included are sections on the new constitutional arrangements including the overview and scrutiny function, the new ethical framework, the community leadership role (including well being power and community strategy) and financial propriety as well as the major implications for local authorities as employers which flow from these changes.

Contributions by leading and experienced practitioners in the field of local government governance make this work necessary reading for all those who either have an interest in or are involved in whatever was in preparing or implementing new governance arrangements for their authorities.

As president of the Association of Council Secretaries and Solicitors I am delighted to have the opportunity of endorsing the work on behalf of the Association.

COLIN G LANGLEY
President – ACSeS
August 2001

PUBLISHERS NOTE

With relation to references to the DETR/DTLR in the text of this work, please refer to the summary of changes to former DETR responsibilities at the following internet address:

http://www.dtlr.gov.uk/changes/index.htm

CW00666074

The Cotton Section of the Agricultural Adjustment Administration, 1933-1937

University of California General Library/Berkeley

Regional Oral History Office

Cully Alton Cobb

THE COTTON SECTION OF THE AGRICULTURAL ADJUSTMENT ADMINISTRATION, 1933-1937

An Interview Conducted by

Willa Klug Baum

Berkeley
1968

ASSOCIATED PRESS PHOTO from Washington Bureau

THREE OF FARM CHIEFS DISCUSS PLANS -- C.A. COBB, Atlanta farm editor, newest appointee under farm act, meets Secretary Wallace of Agriculture and George N. Peek, chief administrator of the wide powers conferred on Wallace to help agriculture. Left to right, Peek, Cobb and Wallace.

W.B. Camp, Willa Baum, Cully A. Cobb.
The day of the interview, 1966.

INTRODUCTION

In May, 1933, Cully A. Cobb was called to Washington, D C., to take charge of the Cotton Section of the newly formed Agricultural Adjustment Administration. Cully Cobb had built his reputation in agriculture, first as an Agricultural Extension work leader in the South, and later as an editor and publisher of agricultural publications. His editorial work had brought him into contact with agriculturalists throughout the country, and he was thoroughly familiar with the problems of cotton raising and merchandising in the South, but less so with the West. Therefore, one of his first official acts was to ask Wofford B. Camp, a California cotton farmer and former Extension experiment station agent, to become his assistant in trying to deal with the chaotic situation facing the cotton industry in the depths of the Depression.

From 1933 to 1937 Mr. Cobb and Mr. Camp worked together on such problems as the cotton plow-up, acreage allotments, gin tickets, and to them most importantly, the prevention of the collectivization of American agriculture.

It was through W. B. Camp that Cully Cobb came to the attention of the Regional Oral History Office.

As part of a series on agricultural history in California, W. B. Camp was being interviewed at length and his remarks on his work with the Cotton Section of the AAA seemed of such significance that, at his suggestion, Mr. Cobb was asked to add

some comments by letter. Mr. Cobb instead offered to come to Berkeley for an interview and on October 26, 1966, both Mr. and Mrs. Cobb and Mr. and Mrs. Camp arrived at the Claremont Hotel for the session. While the ladies went shopping in San Francisco, Mr. Cobb, and part of the time Mr. Camp, devoted both the morning and the afternoon to answering questions on the work of the Cotton Section.

The transcript of those sessions was mailed to Mr. Cobb in Atlanta, Georgia, where he has his business as publisher of the Ruralist Press. Mr. Cobb went over the transcript with great care, making corrections and some additions where necessary. He also added copies of letters he had written to several researchers which went into the same subject in detail. Those letters are appended.

A remark by Mr. Cobb that he had been interviewed by Dr. Roy V. Scott, professor of history at his alma mater, Mississippi State University, led to an arrangement to exchange transcripts of the interviews. A copy of the interview by Professor Scott can be found in the appendix of the Bancroft Library copy of this interview.

The Regional Oral History Office was established to tape record the reminiscences of persons who have contributed significantly to the development of the West and the nation. The Office is under the administrative supervision of the Director of the

Bancroft Library.

Willa K. Baum
Head, Regional Oral
History Office

May 30, 1968

Regional Oral History Office
Room 486, The Bancroft Library
University of California
Berkeley, California

TABLE OF CONTENTS

INTERVIEW I

(October 26, 1966, morning.

Claremont Hotel, Berkeley, California)

Introductory Comments

Baum: I thought you might like to see this book.*

Cobb: I would like to see it.

Baum: Here it is. Here he quotes a letter, "Cobb to author," pp. 1-5. Was that a letter you sent him? It must have been a long one.

Cobb: It was a long one. When you're dealing with men like this, you've got to be sure you do the necessary hedging to try to make it so that they can't quote you out of context.

Baum: Here he's got you quoted. That's from your autobiography.** I think he's got that right.

---

*David Eugene Conrad, The Forgotten Farmers, the Story of Sharecroppers in the New Deal, University of Illinois Press, Urbana, 1965, 223 pp.

(Mr. Cobb had not seen the Conrad book yet. Conrad quoted personal letters from Cobb to Conrad, copies of which are in the Appendix of this interview, and papers from the National Archives, including memoranda written by Cobb.)

**Included in the Appendix of this interview.

Baum: Oh, Mr. Camp, before you leave, I wanted to tell you something that you'd be interested in. I have a list of a lot of people you both know. These people have all given oral history interviews at Columbia University.*

Camp: [Reading from list] M. L. Wilson!

Cobb: Is he still living?

Baum: I don't know. He may be dead, because the Columbia oral history project has been going since 1948.

Cobb: He's dead, I think.

Camp: I better not tell you my opinion of M. L. Wilson. Mr. Cobb can give you his.

[Looking at the list] Cully can give you his opinion of Chester Davis. Poor fellow is still living. He had a stroke recently, and he's not in good shape; and I hate to say anything. But Chester is the man in American agriculture who could sit and look wise and say nothing, and mean nothing...

Cobb: And get further with it.

Camp: And get further with it than any man I knew in America, and knew less about real agriculture. I say that with no reservation.

Cobb: He really knew very little about agriculture.

---

*The Oral History Research Office of Columbia University has interviews with: M. L. Wilson, Chester Davis, Henry Wallace, Rexford Tugwell, Lee Pressman, Harry L. Mitchell, Jerome Frank, Howard Tolley, and Sam Bledsoe.

Camp: I put his brother in the cotton growing business. His mother lived in my town a while too. But Chester was a nice fellow, individually.

Cobb: He was a graduate of some college down in...

Camp: Montana, wasn't it?

Cobb: ...Missouri, I believe. It could have been.

Camp: I don't know. He was editor of an insignificant farm paper in Montana [Montana Farmer] when he was called to Washington.

Cobb: Grinnell College, Iowa, 1911.

Camp: So. Henry Wallace, there's plenty been written, Cully can give you all. Rexford Tugwell: I already, I think, gave you the last two days of his official being in Washington.* Again, I think I told you, Cully was out of town, in Texas or Louisiana somewhere, when Sam Bledsoe--from the Mississippi Delta, Memphis; he's in Washington now... But Sam Bledsoe was the man who came down to the basement and pulled me out of the meeting, and told me. Things happened after that.

Baum: That had to do with Tugwell.

Camp: That's right. Tugwell knew nothing about it, and nobody else did. My conversation with Sam Bledsoe was private. That's the way it was. I told you all through all of these, I had no authority of my own, except as delegated by my boss. [Cobb]

---

*Mr. Camp was in the process of being interviewed for ROHO.

Camp: And he and I thought alike. No matter what I did, if he wasn't there, I knew that was his thinking and he knew that I was going to carry that out. And I never had any fears. I talked just as plainly as if I was the one that had all the authority.

Cobb: When I left town, I handed him the authority.

Camp: Lee Pressman, well, he's one of those that went out with Jerome Frank and that whole caboodle.

Baum: There's Jerome Frank [on the list] too.

Camp: All right. They both went out at the same time. When Tugwell went out, it was some months later.

Baum: He went into the RA--the Resettlement Administration--didn't he?

Camp: He got fired. Or they allowed him to resign. His secretary took the notebook and hid it.

All right. Harry L. Mitchell?

You mean the sharecroppers' president?

Baum: That's right. Southern Tenant Farmers Union.

Camp: Oh! Cully had a lot to do with him. He brought up some folks from Arkansas and Mississippi.

Baum: Tell us about that meeting you had with him.

Cobb: That meeting would be too vague, I think, in my memory to tell you anything about it, except that he was there.

Camp: He brought this group up. Among the ones he brought up was a Negro, a so-called preacher, from down there. Mitchell was

Camp: pressing in a cleaning establishment...

Cobb: Tyronza, Arkansas. He ran a pressing club. They called him "the pants presser."

Camp: When Steinbeck wrote the damnable book The Grapes of Wrath, they were moved in on us, and so on. Then following that, this October 1, 1947, when Mr. DiGiorgio and I had a picket line established for two and a half years, Mitchell was immediately flashed on the national radio as being president of this union, this farm labor union. And he came in here, to California. This was some years after Cobb and I had this experience with him. But it established who he was and what he was trying to do. We knew him to be affiliated with, if not a card-carrying man, we knew what he was.

Jerome Frank, Howard Tolley, Sam Bledsoe...

Baum: I just wanted you to know that all of these gentlemen have given interviews at Columbia University. That's why I want to be sure to get Mr. Cobb on record.

Camp: I don't know about Sam Bledsoe's interview at Columbia, I don't know what they would be--wonderful boy. Never in a spot of personal responsibility there.

Cobb: He was a public relations man.

Baum: Yes, information.

Camp: Information and public relations, and a good boy. But, as I say, I don't know what there would be.

Baum: Columbia University's oral history office has interviews from all the people who were in Washington at a certain time.

Camp: One thing occurs to me right now that is brand new. This is the man who got the information from the horse's mouth that Roosevelt was going to purge Senator George. He can give you the information. I won't. Sam Bledsoe got the same kind of information, that Tugwell was going to use two senators, Joe Robinson and Pat Harrison, and came to me in his [Cobb's] absence. He locked me in my office and said, "You can raise more hell in five minutes than anybody else in town today in a month. And here..." [Fading voices--Mr. Camp leaves the room.]

Baum: Now, let me explain that after we record this, we type it and send it to you for your editing.

Cobb: Be sure that it is what we are trying to say.

Baum: That's why it goes to you. If you want to put it under seal for ten years or so, until everybody is dead, you can.

Cobb: Well, you don't want to hurt anybody. I don't believe that I would be saying anything that would bother anybody much now.

Baum: You can make that decision when you see it. So, if there are certain pages that you want to put under seal, or anything like that, at the time you see the transcript you can make your decision.

Now, I would like to include your biography in this; and

Baum: the letter to Mr. Hornsby, that you sent me a copy of; also, you said you had a copy of the letter to Mr. Conrad.

Cobb: I have the letter to Conrad, and I have the letter to Hornsby. Hornsby's here in California, isn't he?

Baum: Yes. He is the Riverside man. I don't know who he is.

Cobb: I don't know who he is, except I believe he was in the navy, some sort of relationship like that. Then I have the letter of transmittal and some of the material I sent to another boy in Texas. I forget his name now.

Baum: I'd like to include copies of all the letters that you've sent, to make it an official record. Anybody can check it. For instance, this man quotes you, and I'd like to have the letter available so that if anyone wants to see if he quoted you correctly he can come to a library, where a scholar can look at the whole thing.*

Cobb: I have that, and I'll be happy to send it to you.

Brookings Institution Studies of AAA

Cobb: You have a copy of that Brookings Institution study, don't you?**

Baum: Yes. I'll deposit it along with your interview. This was the 1934 copy, by Henry I. Richards.

Cobb: That's the only one they ever printed, that I know of, about the Cotton Program.

---

*All letters mentioned are included in the Appendix.

**Henry I. Richards, Cotton Under the Agricultural Adjustment Act, Developments up to July 1934, Pamphlet Series No. 15, The Brookings Institution, Washington, D.C., 1934, 129 pp.

Baum: There is this other one: Three Years of the Agricultural Adjustment Administration. That's Brookings Institution. I think that's 1937.*

Cobb: I didn't know about that. Did the same man, Richards, do both?

Baum: No, but the same man, Edwin Nourse, was in charge of this 1937 book.

Cobb: Nourse? I knew Dr. Nourse very well. Dr. Nourse and I worked out this particular study--the Richards study--to begin with.

Baum: Nourse was in charge of this 1934 report too, wasn't he?

Cobb: He was in charge of Brookings Institution, and he directed the activities of this man here. [Henry I Richards] This man was on his staff.

Baum: I see. And he [Nourse] got Joseph Davis and John Black to write this 1937 one. I think they were men on the Brookings Institution staff too.

Cobb: I knew Dr. Black, but do not remember Mr. Davis. When was this made?

Baum: That was '34. This was '37. This would be the whole AAA

Cobb: I see. I didn't know that book was in existence. I'll have to get it and see what it says. Does he cover this pretty fully?

---

*Edwin G. Nourse, Joseph S. Davis, John D. Black, Three Years of the Agricultural Adjustment Administration, the Brookings Institution, Washington, D. C., 1937. 600 pp.

Baum: I haven't read it that carefully.

Cobb: Have you read this [Richards book] carefully?

Baum: No, I haven't.

Cobb: Well, this is the one you want to read carefully for the beginnings because this has the organizational activities from the very day that I went to Washington.

Baum: These are fairly technical, but it doesn't include the personalities of the people.

Cobb: They wouldn't do that. That would be outside their field. What they were interested in was just facts stated concisely and accurately. Now, the cotton situation in May, 1933, historically is of greatest importance to your documentation here.

Baum: Would you like to start with that?

Cobb: I'd just like you to quote it. Let me see what it says. It begins on page four. I think you'd have to go back to page one, "The immediate major objective of the Agricultural Adjustment Administration..."* Now, I think you'd almost have to start with that to have your study in relationship to what you are doing for Bill Camp, when he reaches that point in his sketch. This ought to be a part of your recording. [Referring to oral history interview with W. B. Camp]

Baum: We don't come out with any complete study of the Cotton Program.

---

*Richards, Cotton Under the AAA, p. 1.

Baum: We make a transcript of interviews for scholars to use in writing books.

Cobb: Well, anybody who was going to write anything about the Cotton Program would have to start at page one of this 1934 Brookings study.

I knew Dr. Nourse very well and as I now recall I knew Dr. Black. I sat down with Dr. Nourse almost immediately when we were in Washington and I said, "This thing [AAA Cotton Program] is going to do what we want it to do, or it isn't. And I'd like to know why, if it succeeds. And if it doesn't succeed, I'd like to know why, I think the world ought to know why. Let's begin now to make a record." He said, "Do you mean that?" I said, "I certainly do." He said, "It's the first government agent that I ever had approach me that way. It's extraordinary."

I said, "Well, we want to see just exactly what this thing does mean." He said, "All right, then I'll assign this boy Richards." I said, "I'll turn over every record, every thing in the world that he wants to make the most complete study possible." And I said, "What I would expect of Brookings Institution is a completely objective study. Now you assign a man to that task that can approach it from that angle. If it's good, it's good; and if it's bad, we ought to know it. We're going to use a lot of government money and it will be well invested or it will be wasted." That's the why of this particular

Cobb: volume here.

Baum: How did you know Dr. Nourse?

Cobb: I had known him before, in newspaper work. I was an agricultural editor before I went to Washington. I knew the Brookings Institution through him. I knew all of the institutions of that kind more or less intimately because you have to have those in doing editorial work if you are going to cover the economics as well as the political and social aspects of your field.

Baum: You used Brookings Institution studies in your newspaper work?

Cobb: I used their work. It's been revised lately. This was one of the authoritative groups of this kind, and I knew Dr. Nourse and he knew me.

Baum: Had you ever worked with them on putting together one of their earlier studies?

Cobb: No. I had never worked with them. I probably supplied them with data that they didn't have, I don't even remember that now. But something of that kind was probably what brought us together in the beginning. Then I had met him at meetings, at annual conventions, and that kind of thing, up and down the country. That is where agricultural editors are supposed to be when they are trying to prepare themselves to do a better job as agricultural editors.

Baum: In your judgment, the Brookings Institution was doing a good

Baum: job in agricultural statistics?

Cobb: They would do a good job in any field. In any field that they would assign somebody to, I thought that they would do a thorough job, make a thorough study. It would be authoritative, something you could really have faith in. I wanted them to do it, and that was it. This man went right through with the whole thing from the very beginning.

Planning the AAA Cotton Program

Baum: AAA started in May, I think, of 1933. Was it as soon as that?

Cobb: This started right here, when the Agricultural Adjustment Act became a law. I went to Washington in the spring of 1933 to take charge of the cotton program for the southern states. The cotton program covered not only the southern states, but the West as well. The plow-up campaign took place before the Bankhead Act.

Baum: I thought the Bankhead Act was...

Cobb: '34. It became a law on April 21, 1934. We had had a year's activity before it became a law. This tells, I believe, what the original set-up was. The original set-up consisted of myself and J. A. Evans, who was the field agent for the Extension Service in the southern states. That is quoted in my biography,

GETS FIRST CHECK FOR DESTROYING COTTON UNDER RECOVERY PROGRAM

From Left to Right Congressman Marvin Jones, Amarillo, Texas; Cully A. Cobb, E.R. Eudaly, State Administrator, Texas; William E. Morris, Nueces County, Texas; Congressman Richard Kleberg, Corpus Christi, Texas, Seated: President Franklin D. Roosevelt

President Roosevelt today presented the first check, to be drawn in favor of a farmer in payment for cotton plowed under in accordance with the plan to reduce acreage and consequently raise the price of the South's principle crop. The check was for $517 and represents 47 acres which were destroyed by William E. Morris of Nueces County, Texas.

Photo shows the President delivering the check to Morris, who holds a stalk salvaged from the field which was destroyed.

7/23/33

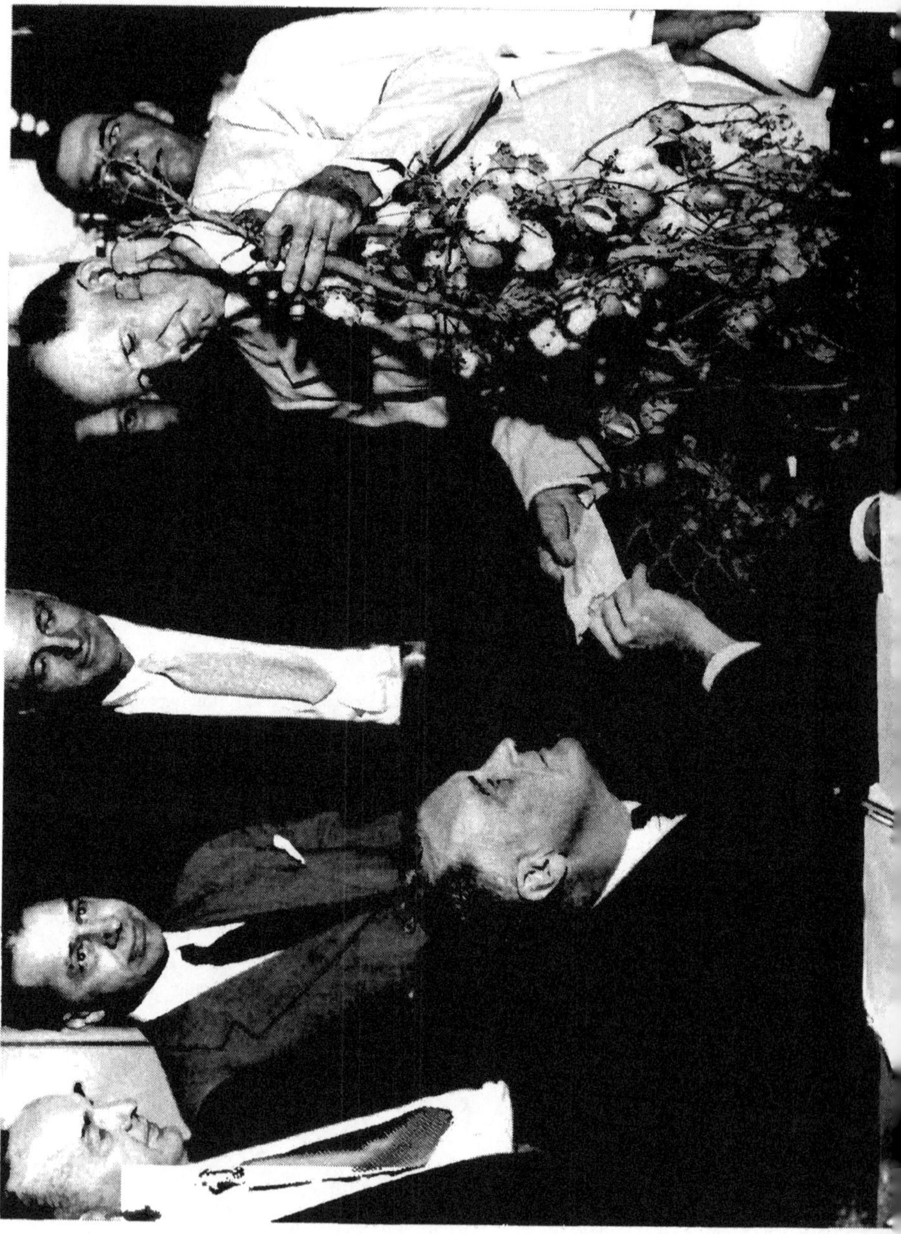

Cobb: I believe.*

Baum: In your biography you quoted J. A. Evans on a meeting where they were not going to use the Extension Service.

Cobb: They were going to eliminate it and set up a completely new organization. They would by-pass the Extension Service, the colleges of agriculture and the experiment stations. They had the most elaborate scheme for a national organization that you ever took a look at. An absolutely astounding thing to anybody that knew anything about agriculture. None of the people that had a hand in this knew anything about agriculture, except the Secretary, of course.

Baum: Secretary Wallace?

Cobb: Yes. But he didn't design it. Tolley had a lot to do with it, but he didn't know a lot about the broad problems of agriculture. He was supposed to be an agricultural economist.

Baum: I thought he came from our University of California Giannini Foundation, didn't he?

Cobb: I don't know where he came from. [Laughter]

Baum: I think Tolley was head of our Giannini Foundation here for just a little while. Then he was called back to Washington and he took a leave. That upset people because they wanted to know whether he was coming back here or if they could appoint

---

* Included in the Appendix.

: someone else.

: I've forgotten that, but I think that's right.

: So you think Tolley was in on writing the original legislation.

: Oh yes. Definitely definitely. Tolley and...

: George N. Peek?

: George Peek didn't have too much to do with it, I think. While he had made quite a success in his business life, he was not really very smart.

He had done a lot in agricultural legislation.

Yes, he had, he had done a lot. But still, I don't think he would deliberately be a party to a subversive thing like this undoubtedly would be, except to approve it. Now Tugwell I do think had a lot to do with it.

This book by Conrad tells who put the AAA together; I think it mentions Tugwell. "Leaders in writing the AAA were Henry Wallace, Rexford Tugwell, Mordecai Ezekiel..."

He had an awful lot to do with it. He (Ezekiel) was an agricultural economist and Henry Wallace's right-hand man.

"...also George Peek, Henry Morgenthau." You didn't think George Peek really had much to do with it.

I don't believe he had much to do with the foundation work, with the thinking that put the original plan together. He probably agreed with a lot of stuff that he didn't have much to do with up to the time he was asked to accept it. I just

Cobb: don't believe he was that type of man. Of course you know a person quite well when you associate with him like that. But I think that's right.

Baum: It mentions Henry Morgenthau here, and General Hugh Johnson.

Cobb: Neither of those had anything particularly important to do with it. I knew General Johnson, and he presided at a few meetings, but pretty soon he was out. Henry Morgenthau was interested in some phase of the cotton industry--cotton handling, I believe. But he, of course, knew nothing about agriculture. He was from New York.

Baum: So these men had no experience in agriculture.

Cobb: No, they had no experience whatsoever, and I don't think they claimed any. Not having claimed any experience at all, they were not in on the basic planning, I believe.

Baum: Then it mentions Bernard Baruch.

Cobb: Bernard Baruch was just interested in whatever went on in the country, but not particularly in this. I've met Mr. Baruch, but I've never had a discussion with him. I think that would tell you that he was not important in the planning back of the Cotton Program or in the execution of the plans that were embodied in the AAA program. He was from South Carolina, and quite a person, a very wonderful person. But he had nothing to do with the program.

Baum: When did you come to Washington? Had the Act already been

: passed--the AAA Act? Were you in on the earlier planning than that?

: I came to Washington in the spring, March--I don't remember the exact day--of 1933. The thing was just being kicked off at that time. I came in because I was supposed to know something about the cotton industry in the South, having been editor of a farm paper with South-wide circulation, and having been graduated from a college of agriculture, also; and having a good many years of Extension work in the heart of the cotton country, where I was supposed to know a good deal about cotton. That was the basic reason I was asked to come in.

It should be added that I was born and raised on a farm, and that my first job off the farm was as a part of a cotton gin crew.

Now, when you were asked, they didn't have the details of the Cotton Program worked out yet, did they?

No, no.

They just had a general outline ..?

No, there was no general outline. There was no general outline of the direction that the Cotton Program took because they had a completely different idea about what the set-up should be What we finally got them to adopt was a complete departure from the original plans, as if it turned right instead of turning left.

Use of Agricultural Extension Forces

: What were some of the specific things that were different?

: Their original plan was to completely by-pass all the agricultural forces that were then in the field. Our plan was to adopt the forces that were in the field completely. That had to do with the colleges of agriculture, and more particularly the Extension forces.

You have to remember that when I went to Washington, cotton had already been planted, and some of it would be ready for harvest in just a very short time. We had to do almost the impossible in a period of sixty to ninety days: get an organization together, get it in the field, and put it to work in a manner that would effect the plow-up program. And we had to take a vote of the cotton farmers on it before we could do it. It was a night and day job. It was just about as hectic as anything could be.

But we succeeded completely in every goal that we set up. And we only did it because we had the good sense, and the President gave us the opportunity, to take over a force that was in the field and in which everybody in the cotton territory had complete confidence. That went for the presidents of the colleges, the Experiment Station directors, the Extension directors, the county agents--both white and colored--throughout

: the entire Cotton Belt and the Vocational Forces. We had an ideal set-up. Use of this ideal set-up was the thing that was so violently opposed by these people, who wanted to set up a completely different program and approach. They wanted nothing to do with it. They wanted land reform, social reform: a revolution, communist style.

: Did they say why they didn't want to use the Extension people already there?

No. It was apparent why, but they were careful enough not to say anything about that.

It would be impossible to get a whole new staff out there in that amount of time.

Completely impossible! That's the thing we had going for us. That is one thing they didn't make a mistake in when they asked me to come in, because I knew them. And also, having worked with every one of these people over a long period of time--twenty-odd years--they knew me, and I knew them, and I think I can say that they had confidence in me, and they were willing to go. They said if this is the approach, why, we're going to go with it.

Do you mean the Extension people had confidence in you, the people throughout the Cotton Belt?

Oh yes. The Land-grant colleges and the Extension people, in particular, had confidence. What we did: immediately, by

: telegram, we had all the Extension directors from the southern states and out here in California come in and work with us on the development of our program and its approach. We knew exactly what we were going to do. They realized very quickly that something of very deep significance was in the wind and this was the thing they were going to have to do if they were going to save Extension work. You'd be surprised at the fear you can read in people's faces when they are up against a threat of the kind that faced them. We had that going for us in our territory. I'm sorry I haven't marked the pages here where I could cite the statements that this man Conrad made with reference to those particular points in our program. And he has given the details of the organization here. That's what I have given all those boys who are using the Cotton Program in writing their theses for degrees.

: I think we should have Mr. Evans' book also.* Is there an article on the work of Extension?

: Well, his is memoirs of Extension work. I have only one copy, I loaned some...

: Is that printed?

---

*James A. Evans, Recollections of Extension History, Raleigh, North Carolina, North Carolina Agricultural Extension Service, Extension Circular no. 224, 1938, 52 pp.

: Oh yes.

: We might have it here in the library.

: I doubt it because I think it was a very limited edition, gotten off, I believe, by the University of Georgia press. You might be able to get a copy through them. I don't know. You could photostat it--the copy I have.

: Is Mr. Evans still living?

: Oh no. He died some time ago. He came back to the College of Agriculture of the University of Georgia as consultant in his last days. A perfectly wonderful gentleman, born and raised in Texas, just as fine as he could be. He knew what it was all about.

He happened to mention this in his memoirs. He went back to the beginnings of Extension work. You probably have that someplace else, when Dr. Seaman A. Knapp was called to Washington and started Extension work way back there in the early days.

: We have some of that. Do you know Claude Hutchison? He was dean of the College of Agriculture here for many years.

: Yes. He's still living, isn't he?

: Yes. He was mayor of Berkeley for a while, after he retired as dean.

: Yes. I knew him and I knew B. H. Crocheron, and I knew Joseph E. Tippett of this group here. Mr. Hutchison came to Washington with the other people when we were giving this kick-off here.

Oh, he did. He didn't tell me about that. We've got a long oral history interview with him and he went back to the beginning of Extension

I think he would tell you about that. Now, he may have sent somebody else, I don't know. But I wouldn't think so on a case that is that important

Well, Crocheron was the head of Extension in California. Crocheron was the head of Extension and Hutchison headed the College of Agriculture. That's right. I don't remember having Crocheron ever show up in Washington; I've met him here on the campus, at the University. He may have sent Tippett, but I don't believe so. Dr. Hutchison did come to Washington and I did see him there. It might have been this occasion, I'm not sure

When you came to Washington, you were going to work on the details of how to run this Cotton Section, which hadn't been established yet. Was it J. A. Evans who was to be your prime assistant?

That's right. We had a little office about as big as this room And he and I were the Cotton Program for the first several weeks. [Laughter] That's all they had.

No wonder you had to use Extension.

There wasn't anybody else' It was just as simple as that.

But Evans says that they were trying to eliminate Extension.

b: It is in his book. He and I sat there until way into the middle of the night, and later, arguing with these people. I just stood up for it, and I said, "We've got to have this, or else we're not going to have any program." And again and again and again I gave them all the reasons why, because I was completely familiar with the cotton situation at that time, in the whole territory, and was able to present arguments that they couldn't knock down. We had to go that route We finally won That's what he (Evans) says in his memoirs and that's in this little biographic sketch

m: Yes. And the description of that meeting is there, and the remark Tugwell made, that he had no confidence in any of the Extension directors.

b: He said that. I was sitting in the Secretary's office, almost as close to him as I am to you, and he said he had absolutely no confidence in Extension forces. I said, "Dr. Tugwell, I can understand that perfectly. The reason is, you don't know anything about them. You haven't had any contact with them, you've had no experience with them. I can understand perfectly well, you haven't. But I've been working with them all these years, and I've been a part of it, and I know who they are. There's not a finer group of people on the face of God's earth. That's the most dependable group in agriculture today Period. He got up and walked out That's when the decision was made.

: He went around behind the Secretary of Agriculture--Evans tells what he said. He patted Wallace on the back, and looking back over his shoulder said in reply to a question by the Secretary, "I haven't a damned bit of confidence in any of them." I don't remember all the language he used, but as Mr. Evans quotes him that is what he said, and stalked out And it was a circumstance of great significance.

But this Brookings study gives you the details of exactly how the program was put into effect, exactly who laid it out from Washington to the remotest community.

Temporary Versus Permanent Program

: To begin with, I think it is important to keep this in mind: it was intended to be a temporary, and not a permanent program. I'll give you this documentary evidence In order to be sure that it was going to be a temporary program, we held to the lowest minimum all of the pay to the committeemen and everybody else that was out in the field to put the program into effect I think we gave the committeemen three dollars a day I had argument after argument over that. They wanted to raise them immediately to the point where they would have an attractive salary, setting up a permanent bureaucracy, with a refusal of

: appointment in Washington, Washington endorsing every one of them, with a salary that would be attractive enough to hold a person in it. We fought that the whole time we were there. Even before that they began to move in on it, making the pay more attractive, and more attractive Now you can see what a bureaucracy does, and exactly what this man (Richards) hints at. He said, "It's good up to now, but we have nothing on which to forecast a future." He believed that it was to be a permanent program. The more important fact in that connection, I think, is that when a government program is started, it usually becomes permanent.

: I don't think people knew that in 1933 as well as they do now.

: I did, that is I felt I did, and hedged against it in every way that we could. I think probably Bill (Camp) told you that. If he hasn't, that ought to be emphasized. In 1934 or 1935 we asked for a 4 per cent decrease in our appropriation, the reason being we wanted to hold our working force to the minimum. You will find this in the records of the House Committee on Agriculture.

: You hedged against any of this program becoming permanent.

: That's right. It was to be a temporary relief program. We were to take it off as soon as we could bring about an adjustment that would result in a fair price for cotton. The first thing to be achieved there, of course, was to bring supply and demand in balance We approached that point very promptly. I

Cobb: don't have the figures in mind, but if you read this again (Richards book) you'll see how the price of cotton went right up immediately after we had begun to bring them to balance. But what we did not want was a permanent program that would regiment the whole cotton industry. That was the original plan before I went to Washington.

Selection of Cobb to Head Cotton Division

Baum: Can you explain why you were selected to head up the Cotton Division?

Cobb: I think it's this: I knew Secretary Wallace very well. He had been an agricultural editor, editor of Wallace's Farmer, and he and I had been in meeting after meeting, had worked together over a long period of time. And I imagine that he just naturally thought of me... I've never discussed it with him. It never occurred to me to do so. It seemed to me, from my point of view, the natural thing to do. I imagine that was what he thought So he cleared it with Senator Russell. Senator Russell told me about it later. He didn't check with me at all. Then he called me up over long-distance telephone and asked me to come to Washington.

Baum: Wallace did?

FIRST PHOTO OF NEW COTTON ADMINISTRATOR

An interesting informal actionagraph of Cully A. Cobb, of Atlanta, newly appointed cotton production administrator under the farm adjustment act, taken today in his office at Washington, a short time after he assumed his new duties.

Mr. Cobb was formerly editor and director of the Southern Ruralist and is a recognized authority of agricultural subjects.

UNDERWOOD AND UNDERWOOD PHOTO 5/23/33

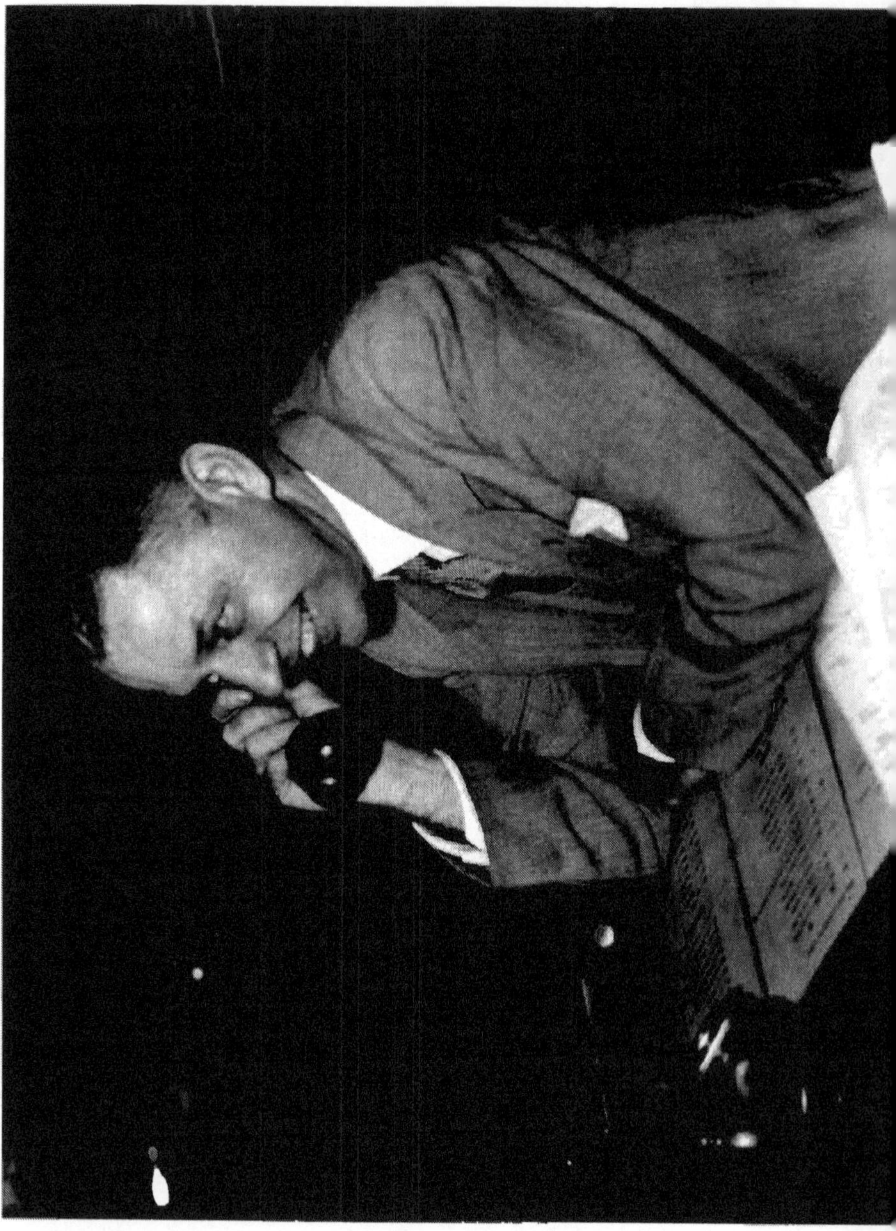

Cobb: Yes.

Baum: So you were the personal choice of Henry Wallace himself.

Cobb: I was the personal choice of Henry Wallace himself.

Baum: Now, your ideas were a little contrary to the ideas of the other people who were working on setting up the AAA.

Cobb: They were completely contrary. They were at right angles.

Baum: Do you think Wallace was aware of the fact that you had a different opinion? Or maybe he wasn't aware of what the whole situation was.

Cobb: I doubt if he was aware of what really was going on. In many ways Wallace was a wonderfully fine person. He was a dreamer, a mystic, and something of a recluse. He was a wonderful mathematician and one of the best Bible students I ever met. Wonderful mentality, but unpredictable. His unrealistic idealism is the thing, I think, that led him to do a lot of things which you can't explain--as witness his ties with A.D.A. and race for President Maybe his idealism was why he invited me to Washington. [Laughter] And though I had always regarded him as basically a socialist, I don't think that he was aware of the extremes basic in all of this.

Then, moreover, Mrs. Roosevelt was having a terrific influence. As a matter of fact, I think she pretty well put the leadership in the Department of Agriculture together at the top. I think you'll find that. She got credit, at least, for

Cobb. running the Department of Agriculture for a long period of time.

Baum. Right there at the beginning, right then when Roosevelt came in?

Cobb: Yes, indeed Right at the beginning I think you have to know that And that is, I am sure, a fact.

But I was answering the question of how I came to be in Washington. I think that's the whole story. I knew Wallace personally, and called him 'Henry.' We were just that intimate--as editors. I had been president of the American Agricultural Editors' Association for a term or two--I think three terms, you can look that up in my biography--and at our meetings we would gather and we would work at the problems that were common to the agricultural press, and you can see how closely that can bring you into contact with the members of the press that are not your immediate competitors. He was in Iowa and I was in the southern states. We had so much in common that brought us together and to an understanding. And I think that's it. It never occurred to me to assign the invitation to anything else other than the fact that we knew each other and our relationship had been cordial. At least I had very great respect for him; I knew what he had been doing with corn, and things like that He was a great student. I think that was it.

Baum: Had you discussed political matters?

Cobb: No, we never discussed political matters because our politics

Cobb: were so patently in opposite fields that we just didn't take up any time with it Strictly agricultural, not political. I don't remember ever having a political discussion with him, except on one point. That was on the pros and cons of states' rights. I wanted states' rights. I don't know for sure that he ever said that he didn't; but at any rate, he wanted to know what I thought about states' rights. I didn't hesitate at all in telling him. That could have been, and of course was of a political nature in a discussion we had.

Baum: Yes, and it might have had some reference as to how you wanted the AAA set up with more local control, also

Cobb: Very definitely. Because what I wanted was every state in the Cotton Program to stand on its own, completely independent, except so far as we had reasonable rules that would regulate their activities I felt, and I'm sure, that was of <u>tremendous</u> importance in the execution of the program. Give each state the opportunity to see what it could do, and it had every other state as a competitor. That gave them the opportunity to move freely and develop freely, the maximum of elbow room for operation. And they did a remarkable job. I was more astounded than anybody else, because of the speed with which we had to put the thing together.

Oscar Johnston and Will Clayton, Advisors on Merchandising

Baum. When you set up your office, you had to get a staff quickly. You had J. A. Evans One of your first men was Oscar Johnston, wasn't he?

Cobb: No, Oscar Johnston was never a member of our staff.

Baum He was the director of the Cotton Pool?

Cobb. Yes, he was the Cotton Pool. We consulted Oscar. He had a good deal to do with helping with the shaping of the programs. But not too much. It would be advice in some particular field He had been in the handling phase of the cotton industry in the South He knew, of course, a lot about cotton production because he was in charge of the Scott Plantation, out from Greenville, Mississippi. He was in charge of that. [Delta and Pine Land Company] It's a big English syndicate.

We never regarded him as an authority in the field of cotton production. But we did regard him, and he definitely was, an authority in the field of cotton sales, merchandising. He was just about the best. He knew the merchandising of cotton as few men that I know. Maybe Will Clayton would know more about it But both of them knew just about the same. Will's from the Anderson-Clayton Company, Houston, you know That's what we got from Oscar, and he was particularly useful, but when he got over in the operations field, that was completely

Cobb: out of his line. He couldn't be of much use to us in that field. But in the other line he was the best you ever knew. I would say this in that connection, that Mr. Clayton worked with us very closely too.

Baum: Oh, he did. He was never in officially, was he?

Cobb: No, he was an advisor on quality, ginning, and packaging. And a completely unofficial advisor. Those of us in the Cotton Belt who knew him had the very greatest respect for Will Clayton, a wonderful citizen and a wonderful person. He knew the cotton business, the cotton merchandising business. He knew it from the farm, from production all the way through, because the quality of the staple begins at the farm, and the man who is going to sell it is interested first in that--quality.

...There was no feeling of inhibition between us and the top management in cotton handling. I could talk to him just as frankly as I'm talking to you. And I knew that I was going to be understood, and I knew that I was not going to be abused, knowing that he would not take advantage of the Cotton Program by doing things for Will Clayton except that he would have liked to see everything done that could be done to improve the industry, particularly at the very beginning, which would mean the quality of the product. He wanted quality first and <u>then</u> he wanted production--quantity. Any man who sells want something

Cobb: to sell. He wanted all the bales of good cotton that could possibly be produced for sale.

Baum: Then he would be against crop limitation, wouldn't he?

Cobb: No, no, he was not against crop limitation. He wanted a balance between supply and demand.

Baum: He would want a good price for it.

Cobb: Yes. He was an economist as well as a dealer in cotton, one of the most alert economists that I know anything about. He knew the whole world as it dealt in cotton. You can imagine how valuable the influence and intelligence of a person like that in business circles could be to the shaping and handling of a program. He was of invaluable service to us, of course, without any official association. That would have been bad for him and bad for us.

Baum: Did he come in and help advise with you in the early days, in early spring of '33 as you were setting up?

Cobb: Yes. I don't remember how soon. I couldn't tell you the dates, but he worked with us from the beginning, I'd say. I'd be safe in saying that. Whether it was one month or two months, or how long, between the day I first got there and the day he first came to town, I wouldn't know.

Baum: I was wondering about people like Will Clayton. He would not be in Washington all the time, and I know in those days you couldn't just jump onto an airplane and hop in for a conference

Baum: like you can today.

Cobb: No, he wasn't there all the time and I never visited him. But they could pretty well get about. They flew then; there was the old tri-motor model Ford, and things like that, and they could get about. But Houston was not too far from Washington by pretty fast train. They had direct communication.

Baum: So people did travel easily then?

Cobb: Oh yes. They traveled very easily then, in light of what they had to travel on. They had a fast train from Houston to Washington, a night and a day.

Baum: So you could get distant advisors to come in.

Cobb: We could get distant advisors. We did not have too many advisors.

Broad Support for the Cotton Program

Ginners and Farm Bureau

Cobb: What we tried to do was to pick those particular persons that fitted into a vital place in an overall program, that is, production and distribution. We simply had to have that to have an over-all program, which gave broad consideration to development, as it must do if your program is going to succeed. You

Cobb: can't grow a lot of cotton for somebody who can't sell it. It can be done, and has been done, that is, you can grow a lot of cotton, and even now it is being done. Because the quality is not the quality the market wants, so it's your cotton--you can't sell it.

Every phase of economics as related to the cotton industry had to have its point of view reflected in our program. Or else we would not have a program that was anything like complete. Moreover, you'd build up so much opposition if you failed to consider everything. And the more the people who were vitally affected knew about the program, the more certain it was that we were going to have the support that we had to have. These people had their agents in every section.

Also we had the support of the ginners. They have ginners' organizations in every state, members of the Southern Ginners' Association. They worked with us. Here and there, we found ginners who did not want any control because they figured that that was not going to give them all the bales that they needed to gin at their gins. But for the most part, they went along. I think that those who were inclined not to go along were pretty well forced into line by those who did know what the program was all about. So, we had pretty good support in that field. Of course, we had the absolute support of every member of the Farm Bureau. All of the southern states had a strong

Cobb: Farm Bureau, and they were working with us on it.

Negro Farmers

Cobb: In order to help meet this outside and inside threat--we knew what was going on, I'd had experience in World War One with the subversives who tried to take over--even at the very beginning, we called in the most intelligent and most influential Negroes in the Cotton Belt to help us with our program. I'm sure Bill Camp's told you about Jim Davis. He had charge of the Negro program of the AAA in the southern states, and he had headquarters at Little Rock. He is one of the smartest men that you ever met in your life. He knew his race. His first job was to meet with the church leadership, by states. The Methodist and the Baptist are the two denominations that 99 per cent of the Negroes belong to. So he met with the Baptist Conventions and the Methodist Conferences and he worked with their presiding elders and local leaders in every state. And in every one of these states all of the Negroes knew the Program through the white and Negro county agents, through our own set-up, and through their preachers. And they explained these programs in every Methodist and every Baptist pulpit in the Cotton Belt.

Cobb: And we've never had a more intelligent and a more loyal group of co-operators than we had with the Negro preachers in the Cotton Belt. Jim Davis was head of it.

Then we brought into the field force Albion Holsey. He was publicity director for Tuskegee. And Mrs. Moton, the wife of Dr. Robert Moton, ex-president of Tuskegee... They were permanent members of our field force. They worked with the county and home agents. Jim Davis also worked with the colored county agents, and the colored workers generally. These Negro women worked closely with the colored home agents. The presence of these Negroes in our force was one thing that confounded my friends in Washington. They couldn't understand why a man born and raised in the South where I was born and raised would be the first to bring these Negroes into Washington.

Baum: What was Jim Davis's background?

Cobb: Jim's father was postmaster in Athens, Georgia, during Reconstruction times, when the carpetbaggers took over. His father was a judge, I think. He was a very, very intelligent person, you need to know that.

Baum: Had Jim Davis had any background in school, agricultural college?

Cobb: I don't remember now what Jim's background was. He was a successful businessman and natural leader.

Baum: I think this book mentions it, maybe you wrote to Mr. Conrad about the work he did. [Looking in index] John Davis?

Cobb: No, John Davis was head of the National Negro Congress. That was a communist outfit. John P. Davis.

Baum: Oh yes. "John P. Davis, secretary of the Washington-based Negro protest organization." That's not the one.

Cobb: No, James P. was the one--our man in Little Rock.

Baum: Conrad doesn't mention him (James P. Davis) by name, but I think he mentions the work with the Negro churches, that the Cotton Program was carefully explained to the Negro people through their churches, so they could understand it.

Cobb: Evidently that was in the letter. But this John P. Davis, I believe his outfit is on the Attorney General's list of subversives.

Baum: That's not the right Davis.

Cobb: No, that's not the right Davis. That Davis did a lot of field work for the National Negro Congress. And on one occasion he asked us for a hearing. He had found a Negro woman out from Florence, Alabama who, he said, had been "brutally abused" by her landlord. So he brought her to Washington and asked for a hearing. E. A. Miller was our hearing clerk, and I attended the hearing. John personally brought this Negro woman in. (Just on the face of it, she was a very fine person. But she had fallen into evil hands.) After she was introduced and the hearing was under way, I turned to her and I called her by name, and I said, "We want to get at the truth of this, that's

Cobb: what a hearing is for.

"You live on Mrs. So-and-so's place?"

She said, "Yes."

I said, "Well, how long have you been there?" And she told me how long, it had been a long time.

I said, "Are you getting along all right, or have you gotten along all right?"

She said, "Yes, sir, we've gotten along all right. My husband died, but we own our mules, we own all of our implements."

I said, "Well, then you're a renter?"

She said, "No, sir, we lease."

Actually the contract was between the lessee and the Department in Washington. The landlord had nothing to do with it.

I said, "Now then, you're a lessee."

She said, "Yes."

And I said, "Now, what's the trouble with it?"

She said, "I got bothered. They told me what Mrs. So-and-so had done wrong to me. We got to arguing. Finally we had a falling-out. And she asked me to leave. I just don't want to leave."

"Oh," I said, "that's the trouble."

She said, "Yes. She's going to take my lease away from me and put me off. If she does, it'll just ruin me."

Cobb: I said, "Well, why in the world didn't you think about this when you were doing all that arguing?"

She said, "Well, I don't know, sir. I just didn't think of it."

I said, "That's the way it was. Let me get your contract and ask you if this is your contract."

She looked at it and said, "Yes, sir."

I said, "That's your name?"

She said, "Yes, sir, that's my name."

I said, "You signed that contract?"

She said, "Yes, sir."

I said, "Well, then you have no complaint, have you? The contract was between you and the federal government."

She said, "Yes, sir."

"Well," I said, "what's Mrs. So-and-so got to do with it?"

She said, "Nothing."

I said, "Well, I'll tell you. There isn't a thing in the world we can do. Because the government, according to this record, has paid you every penny that the government's supposed to pay you."

She said, "Yes, sir, I got it all."

I said, "Now then, what do you want me to do?"

She says, "I want my home back if I can get it."

I said, "I'm sorry that I can't tell you that you can get

Cobb: it back. I don't know, the feeling may have gone to a point where Mrs. So-and-so (and I called her name) won't have you back. But I'll see what I can do."

I worked with the county agent on it, and I don't think she ever took her back. I think the thing had reached the point of irreconcilable bitterness. And maybe the land she leased had already been leased to somebody else. But I think she went out and stayed out.

That was one of the few hearings that we had in Washington. As a case in point, it illustrates one thing: how we were bedeviled by outside agents, who were doing everything under the sun they could to destroy the relationship between the white people and the colored people in our territory. And there wasn't any length to which they wouldn't go. I never could understand why John P. Davis didn't take a little time out to be sure that he had a case. But that was it. Of course, the thing fell flat on its face. He never came back to see me.

But we were discussing the part that Jim Davis and his Negro associates, who were a very definite part of our organization, played in the development of the program and in its execution. We had them right in there sitting with us, so that they would know that what we were saying was what did take place, and so they could say, "Yes, I was there." It means something to be able to say, "I was there when it was done,"

Cobb: when you're talking with people way out at the end of the line.

Baum: Were you ever able to use Jim Davis or these other Negro people in your office to combat the accusations that they weren't being treated fairly?

Cobb: They did most of their work in the field, as a rule. They were called to Washington regularly for conferences. Jim Davis' office in Little Rock was field headquarters for our Negro forces and was fully equipped with all necessary office appliances and secretarial force to handle correspondence, news releases and studies. It was also the center for many conferences.

Baum: I hadn't seen any publicity about them, and I wondered.

Cobb: They did, I'd say, 95 per cent of their work in the field, most of it looking into complaints. Now they had offices in my building also. But their work was in the field, where it was needed most. The loyalty of those colored workers was out of this world. It was one of the most beautiful things in our whole program, to see how they stood by the program itself. They stood by it because they realized that, if the cotton industry couldn't become a profitable industry, they had no place and that nobody else had any place.

We were holding a meeting in Memphis, at the Gayoso Hotel, which was made up very largely of white and colored cotton producers from across the river in Arkansas with some from north Mississippi, but mostly Negroes and white cotton producers

Cobb: from Arkansas where there was much discussion. And we had the hotel full. There was rather a heated argument about some point in the program that one of the Negro leaders did not like. I don't remember what it was now. Obviously he was a plant. One of the Negro farmers from the Arkansas side--I'll never forget him, a tall, stately man--got up and said, "Mr. Chairman, could I have a word at this point?" [They have a way, you know, if you know Negroes, and we knew something was coming.]

He said, "Why, certainly."

And then this Negro said, "I just want to say to my brother, that "if we don't protect the AAA, we ain't gonner BBB."

The audience exploded. And on that note the argument ended

Can you think of anything that would more pointedly or precisely represent a point of view? He said, "We've got to do that."

And what I'm saying is that they appreciated the fact that they had to be loyal to the program, if the program was going to succeed for them or anybody else. But they were loyal, and that's the interesting fact in that connection, and the confounding fact to our enemies. But we had many, many things like that, that represented these little oases in something of a desert. [Laughter] They were very beautiful.

Staff and Administrators

E. A. Miller

Baum: Was E. A. Miller one of your first assistants?

Cobb: Yes. He was the first assistant.

Baum: How did you select him?

Cobb: I knew him. He had been a supervising agent of the Extension Service out of the Washington office, in the South. He was born and raised in Texas and knew the cotton industry. And he was available.

Baum: Did you know him previously?

Cobb: Oh, yes I'd known him for years and years. I knew all the Extension forces, down to many, many of the local county agents, because I'd been out with them in my field work as an agricultural editor. They had driven me up and down the country, every place where there was any particular thing that would represent a point of interest to the whole Cotton Belt. I always went to the state office first. A lot of times somebody from the state office and I would get in an automobile and go to a particular county, and the county agent would pick us up and carry us to see whatever we wanted to see, if it happened to be the Pitchfork Ranch and what they were doing there, or someplace else. So I knew these people from one end of the

Cobb: country to the other.

W. B. Camp

Baum: How did you know W. B. Camp?

Cobb: I knew W. B. Camp to begin with at his Experiment Station down here. We were here near Bakersfield and visited the station while I was president of the Agricultural Editors' Association. The members of this association made a number of study tours and one of them was to our own western country here. We picked up all the agricultural editors at St. Louis. We toured the southern part of the country. Then we came on here and visited the Experiment Station at Bakersfield that Mr. Camp had established.

Baum: That was in the '20's.

Cobb: That would have been '25, I think. It could have been '26. We came in a solid Pullman train, parked the train at Bakersfield. Mr. Harrell was the editor of the paper there, and he, together with the representatives of the Kern County Land Company, was our host You'd know him (Mr. Harrell) because he was a figure in that territory for many, many years.

Baum: The Kern County man.. begins with a J... [Jastro?]

Cobb: I don't know--could have been Jewett. Bill Camp can tell you who he was.

Baum: I'm sure he can, because he worked with that man a lot.

Cobb: I think it was Jewett. [H. A. Jastro--W. B. Camp]

Anyhow, they (Mr. Harrell and the Kern County Land Company) were in charge of our program. It was there that I was introduced to the cotton problem in this territory. We visited the Hoover farm and this whole territory.

Baum: That's the first time you saw Mr. Camp. I don't think he came to Washington for a long time.

Cobb: He came to Washington early in the program, I don't remember the exact date. He came for this reason: I knew the cotton industry from New Mexico east pretty well. But I did not know the cotton industry in the irrigated country, and the only man I knew that did know it was Bill Camp. I felt that we just had to have somebody in there that not only knew it but occupied a position that would let him speak for the territory and its people. And I didn't make a mistake.

Baum: I think that he said that he'd gone back to Washington to present the case of California cotton, which was that they had no cotton history. And the program was based in part on a farmer's five-year history, and a lot of these new farms didn't have a five-year history.

Cobb: I don't remember. That was my introduction to who Bill Camp

Cobb: was. Then who he was is why he was invited into the organization. Of course, he became my "executive vice-president," if you would express it in business terms.

Baum: Did you have any idea that you and he held similar ideas on how to run things?

Cobb: Yes. That was perfectly apparent. There was no doubt.

Baum: I take it you hit it off together.

Cobb Like that. When I was out in the field, I left him with complete freedom to go ahead and sign my name to anything. He observed and honored that freedom very, very carefully. If he ever made a mistake, I don't know what it was. I don't remember, at any rate.

Others

Baum: Was another of your men J. Phil Campbell?

Cobb: No. J Phil Campbell was director of Extension in Georgia. He may have come in as an advisor. We had a group of state advisors. I'm not sure that they were directors of Extension work every time. They in fact were not. But we had an advisory board, and it's entirely possible that Phil was on that board. I wouldn't know now. You'd have to go back and look

Cobb: at the records.

Baum: And W. J. Green?

Cobb: I don't remember him at all. From where?

Baum: I'm not sure. He went out on some investigations or missions for you, I think. Maybe I've got the name wrong. I think I picked it up in that Conrad book.

Cobb: I don't remember him. Some people were sent on missions for us that we didn't send out.

Mary Connor Myers, Investigator

Cobb: We had that Mrs. Myers. I was told she was from Chicago. She was an economist, I think. Bill must have told you about her. Maybe she was a lawyer.

Baum: No, he didn't. I think I read about that in Conrad. Mrs. Mary Connor Myers, isn't it?

Cobb: Yes. And the only mission that she ever went out on that had anything to do with my office was to make an investigation in Arkansas. Of what, I never knew. But, as I have it, she met with groups of people in Memphis and worked in Memphis and out of Memphis, and she is supposed to have made a report. I never saw that report. There's been a lot said about that report. I have no idea in the world what was in it because I didn't send her out to get it. Before she went to Memphis,

Cobb: she came by my office and said, "I'm going to Arkansas to make an investigation, and I'd like to get instructions "

I said, "Mrs. Myers, you are not going for me Of course, I have no instructions for you If you are going to Arkansas, the decent thing to do is to go to the state office at Little Rock and let them know you're there and what you're there for. If you were going for me, you would <u>have</u> to do that You're not going for me."

She turned red and walked out Then some time after that she had finished her work and is said to have sent in a report. I have no idea in the world what was in it, except I am just sure that it would be something I wouldn't like.

Baum: I think that trip was a result of when Mitchell came to see you and he also went to see Secretary Wallace.

Cobb: Could have been. Specifically I don't remember what it was she went down to investigate. You are right. The Mitchell incident sparked it However, when your time is 150 per cent occupied, you don't have much time for that kind of thing, so you just dismiss it And I just dismissed her and forgot her As far as I was concerned, it couldn't ever have been for any good purpose. But she didn't go representing me [Added later in writing by Mr. Cobb] In checking, I find that Green was on one of my committees and was a good man.*

---

* J. Phil Campbell, E A Miller, and W. J Green listed in Conrad as members of an Adjustment Committee to investigate complaints arising from cotton contracts.

Baum: Do you remember that meeting with Mitchell. (H. L. Mitchell)

Cobb: No, I don't remember the confrontation. I just remember that Mitchell came there. That's all. I knew who he was. I knew the radicals he represented. His mission was national publicity and national propaganda. I knew it was part of the plot to discredit the Cotton Division.

Baum: Mitchell came January 1935. And Conrad's book says he talked to you and somebody else was with you. It was H. L. Mitchell, Walter Maskop, and E. B. McKinney. And they were representing the Southern Tenant Farmers' Union. Do you remember that meeting?

Cobb: I just remember that we had a meeting and what its purpose was. I believe it was at that meeting that representatives of the National Negro Congress picketed our Washington office. This organization was led by John P. Davis and is on the Attorney General's list of subversive organizations.

Baum: Then it says that after that Secretary Wallace, I guess, sent out Mrs. Myers.

Cobb: I don't know who the individual was that sent her out--that authorized the trip. I don't believe Wallace sent her out. Somebody else down the line did it. Maybe Paul Appleby, or Alger Hiss, or Jerome Frank.

Baum: This had something to do with the landlord-tenant relation.

Cobb: That would be what she would go for, definitely. It would have to be based on some alleged landlord-tenant problem.

[The following questions were mailed to Mr. Cobb at the time he corrected the manuscript and he replied in writing.]

Baum: There have been many questions and surmises as to what happened to the Myers report, which has never turned up in the records of the AAA. It was turned over to Chester Davis in March, 1935, at which time there was much public furor in the press about its being suppressed. Could you comment on why the report was not opened to anyone at that time and what might have become of all the copies of it? Mr. Cobb, as there is so much about this Myers report, including the suspicion that you had it destroyed, could you comment on this for the record?

Cobb: Yes. Following my promise, and for the record, I am glad to comment more fully on the Myers incident. I realize that the comments I have already made on this incident have left a lot unsaid. And I also realize, when I look at some of the answers I have given, that I could be accused of using a convenient memory to forget facts that might be embarrassing if put into the record. So I am really glad to comply with your suggestion that I make a fuller statement for the record.

First, I will have to accept it as a fact that Mrs. Myers did go to Memphis, Tennessee, and probably to Arkansas, that she did make an investigation, that she did submit a report, and that the report had to be either good or bad. I have always assumed that it was bad, that indeed it was very bad. It would have to be bad if it reflected the violent claims of the Southern

Cobb: Tenant Farmers' Union and its fellow travelers in and out of Arkansas. To better understand this whole episode, it should be stated that the effects of the depression of the late 20's and early 30's had been very severe in this area of big plantations and many tenants as well as in many other areas throughout the Cotton Belt. Widespread suffering and uncertainty was the natural result. These were among the primary reasons why this area was selected as the most favorable place in the whole South to start a revolution. The revolt here was to open the way for the original program of radical social reform and have it take the place of the AAA program in effect. The Southern Tenant Farmers' Union, an ultra-radical, communist-infiltrated, bi-racial organization, with headquarters in Tyronza, Arkansas, headed up by a white man, formerly connected with a drycleaning establishment, took over at this point. The activities of this organization, which had the blessing as well as the active assistance of Norman Thomas, John P. Davis of the National Negro Congress, and doubtless many other radicals and radical groups, were, of course, aimed at creating the violent discord and hatred between whites and blacks and more especially, between tenants and landlords necessary to get their revolt going.

Frankly, whether she knew it or not, I am very sure Mrs. Myers represented our bitter enemy, the communist cell there in the Department of Agriculture in Washington, in this assignment.

Cobb: It was to be a frontal attack upon the Cotton Program. Such a visit to Arkansas undoubtedly had been planned for a long time and in the strictest secrecy. Also, it had certainly been planned with great care for all details, especially for strategy.

The Southern, or Cotton Division, was not only not consulted but we knew nothing of the plan until Mrs. Myers visited my office and announced that she had been selected to make an investigation in Arkansas. As I have indicated already, I told her in no uncertain terms that she was not representing me, nor the Cotton Section, and that I had no instructions for her. I have always assumed that those who did send her were afraid that we of the Cotton Section would try to stop the investigation if we knew about it. Our attitude when we found out about it was that they could make any investigation they pleased. The fact is, we would not have cared less and would not have stopped it if we could because we knew she was going into a hotbed of communist activity and that somebody was going to get badly burned.

From the very beginning, when we sat in the presence of the communists and fellow-traveling radicals in Washington, we were fully aware of their bitter hostility to the program adopted, and we took pains to prepare our forces in the field and elsewhere for just such an eventuality as this Myers

Cobb: episode. The most vital preparation for such an eventuality was written into the body of the contract cotton farmers signed with the government. Nothing was left undone in drafting these contracts to see to it that they covered every detail of operation in a manner that would secure justice to tenants of every type and landlords of every type. And in the much broader sense these contracts were drawn with full regard for our broad civic and moral responsibility. What I mean by full regard for civic and moral responsibility is this--many tenants had been on the farms where they lived for many years. The contract required the landlord to keep the same number of tenants and not only permit them to use land, that normally would have been planted in cotton, to grow their gardens and produce feed for home consumption; that is, for chickens, a cow, and hogs for their meat, they were also to be permitted the free use of farm implements and mules and the continued free occupancy of the houses they lived in. While this would be considered as normal procedure among farmers, we felt by putting it into the contract, it would answer a lot of questions from meddlesome outsiders before these questions were asked. It would also let the tenants know that they and their welfare were much in our minds.

Beyond the contract was the selection of outstanding farmers as local committeemen to supervise local activities. Because of radical activities over a long period of time in some

Cobb: areas of Arkansas, and as indicated, the nature of farming in this area, this territory was selected as the starting point for the planned revolt.

The next we heard of Mrs. Myers, it was reported that she was in Memphis and that she had set up headquarters there for her investigation. I do not know that this is true, but I assume it to be a fact. None of us ever made any inquiry about her. We felt sure we would know about her activities soon enough.

Following a personal complaint by John P. Davis, President of the National Negro Congress, the visit of a delegation of the leaders of the Southern Tenant Farmers' Union, the picketing of my office, and other incidents in Washington shortly before Mrs. Myers' departure for Memphis, or Arkansas, I feel sure that many conferences were held to plan such action. No doubt they were attended by John P. Davis, Norman Thomas, and the officers of the Southern Tenant Farmers' Union. It is not at all unlikely that Brooks Hays, ex-congressman from Arkansas and one-time president of the Southern Baptist Convention as well as many others of like mind, were in attendance. It should be pointed out here that the National Negro Congress and the Southern Congress for Human Welfare are on the Attorney General's list of subversive organizations. Out of such a conference would come a comprehensive plan for the investigation, detailing exactly how Mrs. Myers would proceed, where she would go,

Cobb: whom she would see, and what she would look for.

Finally in time Mrs. Myers returned to Washington and made a report That is what I heard and assume that is what did happen. And as indicated, the report had to be good or bad. I have always assumed that it was bad, probably very bad. It would certainly have dealt in extremes of condemnation if it reflected the claims of the Southern Tenant Farmers' Union and its fellow travelers in and out of Arkansas. To whom she made the report, I do not know. I never saw it. In fact, I never talked to anybody that had seen it. I have always felt that such a report would start out by blaming the Program and more especially the landlords for all troubles, especially the troubles of tenants. For its purpose such a report would have to deal in extreme claims of criminal abuse of tenants by landlords, and complete unconcern, if not criminal neglect of the rights of tenants by the Washington office of the Cotton Division. I had also always felt that that sort of report would naturally be brought in by a representative of the sort of group that sent Mrs. Myers to Arkansas and as already indicated, that it would be so violent that when published it would immediately call for a Congressional investigation. Naturally such an investigation would start in Washington. And one angle would have led straight to the White House. I don't think those who were responsible for Mrs. Myers' trip to Arkansas

Cobb: had thought of that until she showed up in Washington with her handiwork and they had had a look at it. I would not only have welcomed an investigation by Congress but would have asked for it. However, the bonfire that was to light up the skies from coast to coast revealing the "vile fruits" of the Cotton Program and the villainy of those of us who were in charge of the Program, was undoubtedly discovered to have been built of material that would have blown up in the faces of those who built it if they had dared to strike the match

While nothing but the report itself would make me believe it was not bad, there, of course, is a very, very remote possibility that the report was so-so, or maybe good. However that may be, there was still no bonfire

Out of our own investigations and the constant vigil of our own local officials, we knew what the situation was. And this is not to say that there were no serious clashes. There were serious clashes. They were the inevitable, indeed intended result of the vicious efforts of those who had been going up and down the region, preaching hatred and urging revolution. Under the urging of these agents of hatred, some of them bitter enemies of our way of life--the communist agents, especially--much bad feeling was created and there were a good many cases of violent disputes that forced landlords to drastic action. And violent conflict was the goal. It was what the movement

Cobb: was organized for. And it is amazing that there really was so little trouble.

As a matter of fact, the Southern Tenant Farmers' Union never grew beyond a very small area in eastern Arkansas. Its dreams of national revolt and the dreams of its stand-by organization, the Southern Conference for Human Welfare, were crushed by the success of the AAA program they had hoped to wreck. Even so, it did give us a lot of trouble around Tyronza, Arkansas, where it was born. The fact is, however, it folded before the Attorney General even had a chance to classify it. Had he done so there is not the slightest doubt that it would promptly have been placed in his list of subversive organizations. [End of written comments.]

Baum: Did Wallace ever talk to you about that? I don't mean this investigation, but the landlord-tenant problem. Was that something that he took an interest in or not?

Cobb: No, no more than any other problem that confronted him. He left that pretty well to us. He personally never intervened and never interfered so far as my memory goes now. He left that to somebody further down the line. He may have authorized it, just in the course of business, as he would authorize anything else, without even knowing what it was. But so far as instigating it himself, no! I'd say no, he didn't do that.

George Peek and Chester Davis

Baum: Chester Davis must have been administrator at that time.

Cobb: He was administrator part of the time. George Peek was then...

Baum: Tolley?

Cobb: No, Tolley was not in. Somebody else, I can't think of his name now. But Chester was administrator when I resigned and went back to Atlanta. He probably was administrator when this thing happened.

Baum: I thought it was George Peek, then Chester Davis, then I know Tolley became administrator; but there may have been someone in between there. We'll have to check our history on that. I'm pretty sure Chester Davis succeeded George Peek.

Baum: I think George Peek resigned in December, '33. So he wasn't there very long.

Cobb: No, he wasn't there very long.

Baum: Was George Peek a good man to work for?

Cobb: He didn't bother us at all.

Baum: They pretty much left the Cotton Division to you?

Cobb: Yes.

Baum: George Peek did. How about Chester Davis?

Cobb: Well, Chester belonged to a group, and that group was the group that gave us so much trouble.

Baum: You think Chester Davis belonged to that group?

Cobb: Ideologically?

Baum: I had gotten the idea from that Conrad book that he was kind of middle-of-the-road.

Cobb: He was kind of in the middle-of-the-road, yes. But Chester didn't bother us too much, except when something like this other thing came up and he got word about it. He was quite nervous, you know, and he'd get excited about things like that. But Chester pretty well let us have our own way. He could have given us a lot of trouble if he had been disposed to swing too far away from the ideals that we held. But he didn't. We never fell out. As far as I know, I was never his enemy, and he certainly never was mine. We got along all right, probably because there was not too much interference with our Program. Chester had respect for me. He may not have liked me an awful lot personally, and he may not have liked Bill Camp an awful lot personally, but he had respect for the fact that we knew what we were working with and had demonstrated, certainly, in the early days of the Program, that we did know what we were working at and we knew the cotton industry and we had the confidence of the people--I think that probably was the thing that influenced him most--also the confidence of the representatives in Congress. I knew them all, the senators and the representatives, and kept them informed.

Baum: Were you as close to E. A. Miller as you were to Mr. Camp?

Cobb: Oh no. Because it was a night and day association with Camp and me, but just the normal executive contact with a man in a department with Miller.

Mechanizing Check Writing for Benefit Payments to Farmers

Baum: I think one of your big problems was getting out those checks.

Cobb: [Laughter] The first check that was ever automatically written and signed by the federal government went to pay William E. Morris, a cotton producer in Neuces County, Texas. He was the first man that got any pay in the early program. They (the U. S. Treasury) had bogged down so completely that they said they were not able to move. And we got IBM to come in and set up a complete check-writing system. And brother, when we got to the point where we could write checks, they went [tap, tap, tap] like that. And we caught up pretty soon with the problem of getting these checks out. But you would be surprised at the fight.

We had to fight Treasury. Treasury said that the only way you could write a check that couldn't be forged was to sign it by hand. Well, Senator Bankhead and the balance of the senators and congressmen from the territory went to the Secretary and to the President and said, "Listen, we're going

Cobb: to get these checks out." So they got the checks out.

A funny thing happened in that connection. I didn't know any better, so I got a photographer to come in and make pictures of that first check. [Laughter] I had a secret agent come up to see me in a day or two who said, "Have you got a copy of the picture of that check?"

I said, "What?"

He said, "Have you got a copy of the picture of this check we made to this man at Corpus Christi, Texas?"

I said, "I've got several of them."

He said, "Well, don't you know that's a violation of the law?"

I said, "I do not," and I did not.

He said, "Can you find all those pictures?"

I said, "I think I can. I'm sure I can."

He said, "Well, brother, dig them up."

I reached in the desk and pulled them all out and handed them all to him.

He said, "We'll burn them. That is definitely a violation of the law. Boy!"

I said, "Now, how come the Department of Agriculture let me get somebody to make those pictures? Everybody knew all about it."

He said, "Well, everybody violated the law then."

Baum: I know there's a law against photographing money.

Cobb: That was money. That was the photograph of the first check that was ever mechanically written by the federal government. It was written on July 14, 1933--just about four months after I went to Washington!

Baum: Now, you must have had to expand your staff awfully fast to handle all this--deciding how much to pay everyone, and all that.

Cobb: We did E. A Miller helped us a lot with that. And Mr. Camp helped us a lot with that, and Mr. Charles Alvord. He was our controller. A perfectly marvelous man in that field. Together with the rest of us, we were able to set up a clerical group there that performed miracles, almost overnight.

Baum: That's what it seemed to me. You had to get those checks out in the summer of '33, didn't you? You got going around May.

Cobb: There were plenty of people available. Remember what the situation was. Unemployment was at a record height. So, what we had to do was screen them. It was not a matter of availability. And we brought in people from the states whenever we could because they could then go back to the states and report what was going on. But we had a marvelously efficient clerical group. We had a stenographic pool, and all that. That was developed in a period of about five months. We had <u>some</u> setup, and very, very efficient. But we got the checks out. We

Cobb: never would have been able to break the Treasury loose from its hide-bound tradition of signing, I believe, six or eight checks at a time with a pen, however many there were, without the force of an emergency. It got to the point where they couldn't do anything about it. We brought IBM machines in and signed those checks and got them out.

Elections, Contracts, and Compliance Committees

Baum: Was it hard for you to get the farmers to sign the contracts in the first place?

Cobb: Not at all. We had elections every year and a very efficient field force.

Baum: Well, right in '33 you were faced with the problem of plow-up immediately.

Cobb: Yes. And we had to get out and get a vote on it before we could put a plow in the ground. And this study by Henry I. Richards gives you the details of that. It was an overwhelming sign-up. I don't think anybody in Washington ever believed it could be done; they said it was just impossible, the farmers are not going to do it. But they did do it And they plowed up their cotton too, 10,495 acres of it. Each one was assigned a quota The faithfulness with which they carried out that program is

one, I think, of the highest testimonies to the integrity of a group of people that you will find anywhere in the records. They did what they said they were going to do--plow up ten million acres of growing cotton with a prospective yield of over four million bales of cotton.

Here and there, there were some that fudged. But I'd say 99 9/10 per cent did what they said they would do. Those who did more than they were expected to do made up any possible shortage due to those who were willing to cheat.

: By '34 and '35 you had appointed compliance committees locally.

Yes, long before that. All of the committees that had to do with the program in the field were local. And our local compliance agents were selected by the producers in a territory for their integrity and the fact that they knew about cotton So we just eliminated a million problems at one stroke, in selecting that type of person. You can understand what a terrific foundation of integrity that builds under your whole program Everybody trusting that whatever he said was right, why, that was it

If anything happened in a community so that anybody needed to be told that he wasn't doing what he ought to do, he was told And compliance was met. We had a minimum of that kind of problem. You would expect some of it, naturally. A person wouldn't want to go along,and if he did go along he

Cobb: wouldn't want to do all that he was supposed to do. We'd have somebody wait on him from his own community, a committee of one or two or three, and say, "Now listen " You get compliance, and you get it in the right spirit. And it wasn't somebody coming down from someplace high up to tell him what to do They settled the problem in their own communities. We just had a minimum of difficulty at that point. Nothing ever to worry about.

Baum: Were there any people that would come out from your office directly, not local people, if there was some criticism of the local committee?

Cobb: I'm sure there must have been I do not remember an occasion for it now But I'm sure there must have been

Baum: I guess I've read some articles that there was some criticism, that the local committee would overlook some non-compliance by a friend, that there was a little bit of favoritism there, which I suppose is a problem with a local committee as well as having community support.

Cobb: There might have been, but I don't know about it. I knew of no flagrant case. I had complaints, like everybody else had. But when I looked into them, as a rule, they fell flat, or compliance had been properly completed A lot of times things like that come out of a misunderstanding rather than a violation in fact. They just didn't always understand what they and their neighbors were supposed to do and thus made their

Cobb: complaint When they were told what they should have done and what they had done was all right, they felt all right We had a super-abundance of complaints by agitators, or due to their activities, but that is not what we are talking about here. But we didn't have much misunderstanding because our program was completely presented in every detail. We tried to make sure that every cotton producer knew everything there was to know.. It was pretty complicated, but it was presented to all cotton growers, white and black, in every schoolhouse in every community. They weren't asked to accept something that they didn't understand They were asked to come together and to stay together until they knew what they were doing. That's exactly what they did That's why we got compliance as we got it and why we got such an overwhelming vote of confidence when they voted whether to go along with the program or not

Baum: This book--Nourse is not the main author, but he's listed--* says that in the AAA, the idea was to try to get the local farmers to help work out the program, and they got more initiative in helping work out programs and carrying them out in the

---

*Edwin G. Nourse, Joseph S. Davis, and John O. Black, Three Years of the Agricultural Adjustment Administration, The Brookings Institution, Washington, D.C., 1937

Baum: Midwest, in the corn, hog and wheat programs than they did with the southern farmers

Cobb: I don't quite see how that could be. At the beginning the Extension directors in the northern states were very reluctant to go along until they realized that there was a plan afoot to completely bypass Extension work and set up a duplicating force under completely new leadership with headquarters in Washington. However, I doubt that is what is meant in the comparison. It could have referred to co-operation or lack of co-operation as between the farmers in regions where crops overlapped, as in the case of corn and hogs, the great commercial crops of the Middle West However, almost before the other programs got under way, the South had already made an enormous contribution to the adjustment of the corn and hog situation and in fats and oils. Mr Richards puts it this way on page 78 and 79 of his book. "While the southern market for feed, food crops and products produced in other parts of the United States may have been reduced somewhat by this program, an offsetting factor was the destruction of a potential crop of about 1.9 million tons of cottonseed. This quantity of seed will usually yield about 295,000 tons of cottonseed oil (the equivalent of approximately one fourth of the lard produced in the United States), 850,000 tons of cottonseed meal and 500,000 tons of hulls "

This all happened between March and Christmas in 1933 and

Cobb: does not take into account the southern contribution of similar character and proportions in subsequent years Mighty little publicity was ever given to these facts And even though they could be regarded as a byproduct of the Cotton Program, they were just as real and just as effective as if they had been a main objective in crops and food products adjustment in the Middle West. And it is easy to see that there would be some difficulty in fitting these contributions of the cotton farmer into a national program As a matter of fact, I do not believe there was ever any attempt made to do that in working out the corn and hog and other programs. And I do not believe our farmers ever fussed too much about it. They just remembered it

What I was talking about is discussing co-operation and what I had in mind was co-operation as between cotton farmers and our forces in Washington. I do not see how a greater percentage of co-operation could have been secured in any programs. Consequently I feel that what you refer to was in a wholly different field. And I would accept the Brookings Institution statement as squaring with the facts as they found them. Even so, I was never conscious of any lack of co-operation between those in charge of the Cotton Program and those in charge of other programs. And in working out the Cotton Program, as it related to soil use, we took pains to see to it that the

Cobb: corn and hog and other programs were protected.

Baum: You feel that you got good co-operation from the southern farmers?

Cobb: We got, I'd say, the maximum.

Baum: Did they help in working out programs?

Cobb: Yes, they, the farmers themselves, helped in working out programs in their community meetings. They helped in working out programs in this way: when they came together to study what we were presenting, as a preliminary program, they brought up their objections and their discussions and, if we hadn't covered a point, you can see how tremendously helpful an individual could be who is so vitally interested as the man whose life and blood is at stake. So we got plenty of help. The more highly intelligent producers were there in complete representation. We didn't have trouble on that point, though

Baum: It's almost twelve o'clock. Would you like to break for lunch?

Cobb: All right... In the meantime you can think of other suggestions.

Baum: Here is the book by Conrad.

Cobb: Yes, I want to get a copy of this book and I want to get the records back in hand that I sent the man because I'm out of duplicates of those now, out of this Cotton Under the Agricultural Adjustment Act. (Richards) And I'll send you a copy of the letter of transmittal that I sent along to Conrad with the Richards' book itself.

Baum: I'd be interested, if you get a copy of that Conrad book, if you agree or disagree with certain points or pages of it

Cobb: Dr. Scott at Mississippi State was telling me about this book.

I said, "Who wrote it?"

He said, "Conrad."

I said, "Yes, I sent him a lot of material."

He said, "I don't think you'll like his book."

I said, "That's neither here nor there. I want his book to see what he said because I sent him this material and I want to see how much of it he used."

INTERVIEW II

(October 26, 1966, afternoon
Claremont Hotel, Berkeley, California)

Purge of AAA Liberals, February 5, 1935

Comments on What Happened and Why

Camp: ...the President said there would be no legislation. None Old Cotton Ed, and Driver, and Joe Robinson, all of them said that. But I was clear about Cully Cobb. He was in Texas I knew what I was doing at all times.

Cobb: She knows what the proposition was that they were fired over.

Camp: ...Chester One thing Cully Cobb picked up the telephone many years after that in Atlanta and called me and he said, "You'll get a kick out of an article in the paper."

I said, "What is it?"

"Chester Davis claiming credit for firing that bunch."

Of course, he and I know the facts

Baum: This is what you say is the lie: "Davis dismissed "

Camp: Davis was going to be fired that same day, I happened to know. He didn't know I knew. That same bunch of liberals were going to get him. And they found out that Cully Cobb had more power than some of them, so they knew that Hell would be poppin'.

Cobb: Anyhow, Chester Davis was sent to Europe immediately. When he got back he was a member of the Federal Reserve Board.

Cobb: The only case I know of Chester Davis trying to fire anybody was that he came to me one day and said, "You've got to fire Bill Camp."

I said, "O.k., fire me first."

Baum: Why did Chester Davis want to get rid of Bill Camp?

Cobb: [Laughter] He wanted to get rid of me too. He didn't want to get rid of Bill Camp any more than he did me, because we just didn't fit in his organization.

Camp: Get 'em one by one, Cully, pick 'em off one at a time.

Baum: Mr. Camp, what about this part here: "Wallace decided to side with Chester Davis because he thought the re-interpretation of Paragraph 7 was bad law." This indicates that Davis was against the re-interpretation of Paragraph 7. You say that's not true [Reference here is to statements in Conrad, p. 147]

Camp: That isn't what I said. I said that when he says that he fired these people, that's the lie He had nothing to do with that.

Baum: Yes: "Davis dismissed Jerome Frank..." This was why I asked you about Davis It sounds like Davis disapproved of this re-interpretation of Paragraph 7.

Cobb: He didn't have guts enough to come out and say so.

Camp. If he did, I didn't know it. Period.

Baum: So I think that this book certainly gives the wrong idea then.

Baum: Because you get the idea that Davis was the one who opposed this re-interpretation, and that he took it to Wallace and pointed out the way Jerome Frank and his group had re-interpreted it; so Wallace went along with Davis and told Davis to fire the whole bunch.

Cobb: Well, Jerome Frank had a way of trying to administer a program as well as legally interpret it. I took a document in to him to sign one day, and he didn't sign it. In two or three days I went back and insisted that he sign it; I had to get it out. He wrote a note at the bottom, "Signed for legality but not for policy." That was Jerome Frank. And that's the position that they took a lot of times. Undoubtedly it was the same thing here. The thing that was involved here was involved there, they wanted to make their interpretation not legal but administrative.

What he was going to do was to dictate to me what the administrative procedure was, regardless of law. He said, "Legally that's all right, but that's not what I want."

I said to him, "I'm not interested in what you want administratively. Is it legal?"

Efforts to Discredit Cotton Division

Baum: I know there were efforts to discredit the work of the Cotton

Baum: Division. One of those you mentioned to me before I turned on the tape. Could you repeat that now? It concerned a press release about some girl who was beaten for opposing cotton landlords Could you add in here the Mamie Sue Blagden case? Do you by any chance have a copy of the article that could be Xeroxed for inclusion as a sample?

Cobb: The article appeared as a feature in Time magazine. And was illustrated with a number of pictures. One showed wide black "bruises" on Miss Blagden's buttocks--supposed to be the result of a "beating" in Arkansas. True or not, dirty remarks about Mamie Sue and ridicule in general quickly hushed this up I never heard of her again.

Baum: What were you saying about Secretary Wallace being easily fooled?

Cobb: In many respects, he was the most naive man that I ever knew These clever designers could put almost any sort of a scheme over on him, even if they adversely affected his most trusted workers. For instance, I fired a man by the name of Victor Pryor, who, I was told later, had been an employee of the federal government, in a Land Bank, as I remember, that had been let out for some cause. How he got into the Southern Division, I do not know. Anyway, very soon after he became an employee of the Cotton Section, he got mixed up in some sort of a mess in Texas and I fired him. I had forgotten at the time that if you do not dismiss an employee with prejudice, he

Cobb: can be rehired.

Camp: You got him fired because I had to make a trip out to College Station, Texas right quick And I found out a lot of crooked stuff and telephoned you right back.

Cobb: And out he went, because of what Bill found out.

Cobb Well, of course he loved me after that. A little bit later he came in with a story that Bill Camp and I were getting rich selling gin tickets. Of course he came to those who wanted to get rid of Bill and me. And it was undoubtedly upon their urging that Wallace authorized an investigation

In the Program, we issued permits, in the form of gin tickets, to producers to permit them to gin so many bales of cotton. And a ginner couldn't accept his cotton unless he had a ticket to go with it. In some areas they didn't make enough cotton to take up their tickets and we gave them the privilege to sell from Texas to South Carolina, or Georgia, for instance, or anyplace else--up to a certain amount. In one of the counties in southeast Texas--Nacogdoches County, Texas--he alleged that Bill and I were selling these gin tickets and making money hand over fist

They came to me and told me that they were going to investigate this; what they had found out, and that they were going to have him (Pryor) go down there. They sent him down there, and he took his secretaries along. They belonged to

Cobb: the Mamie Sue Blagden class. He got all his figures together--he had checked everything--and then he brought them all in to Washington The solicitor general of the Department of Agriculture had come to me in the very beginning and told me what they were doing I said, "Just go right ahead and let him (Pryor) make the investigation. I have no objection to it at all."

Well, he said, "You have no objection?"

I said, "Absolutely none in the world You just encourage him to make it just as complete as he possibly can "

Well, he made it complete, and when the results of the investigation came in and everything was laid before them, they came over to my office and said, "Well, these are the serial numbers of tickets you are accused of selling "

I said, "O.K."

Mr. Alvord was our controller. He did all of the accounting We handed the report over to him and said, "Mr. Alvord, what about this?"

He looked at them, the serial numbers, and said, "Well, yes The tickets bearing those serial numbers have been destroyed, they've been burned "

Those tickets had been called in and burned in the presence of witnesses. The solicitor in his findings said, "The evidence shows that Bill Camp and Cully Cobb have shown due diligence in the performance of their duties and are to be thanked."

Twenty thousand dollars was set aside to conduct the

Cobb: "investigation." How much more was spent I do not know. They were sure they had us where they could put us both in the penitentiary That was just one instance of harassment So far as we (Bill Camp and I) were concerned, it was all in the day's work And Wallace was a victim of his friends, Bill and I were victims of both.

Baum: About when was that? Was that before or after the purge?

Cobb· That would be in 1935 or 1936.

Camp: It was after this purge.

Cobb: It was after, way after this purge

Baum: That purge was February 5, 1935. That was the day everyone got fired. It was after that. Somebody was still after you.

Cobb: I met Chester Davis in the hall one day, and he said, "Cobb, what's happening to you? They haven't made a drive on you this week " [Laughter]

Camp· Mrs Baum, no two men in history have ever gone through Hell like this man and I did.

Baum: They were really out to get you both?

Camp: Oh yes And neither one of us was there for a job. We'd both been drafted That's what hurt.

Baum: Did they try any other ways to get you?

Cobb: None so glaring as that, but they tried other ways--rumors about big jobs being offered you, etc., etc.

They tried to get Bill mixed up with a woman One of the

Cobb: men in my department came in one day and said that they have got this started on Bill now to put him out. He said the story is this: on a certain day at a certain hour, Bill is supposed to have made an improper proposal to Mrs. So-and-so in the stenographic pool.

I said, "O.K., let's make the investigation."

They came in and made the investigation as to dates and all, and wanted to know about it from me, looking at the date and the hour.

I said, "O.K. Bill was out of town. And it just so happens that I was in the stenographic pool exactly at the hour and the minute that you say he was there. And he was not there." They tried to ruin him in his home life and every place. Oh, boy. But that was that.

Camp: There are a couple of other things I had to tell you. I didn't have to tell you that because they tried to make it dirty.

Cobb: What I'm telling you isn't dirty. It just wasn't true.

Baum: Different ways to try and get rid of someone.

Cobb: And that is a common trick there too. You have to know about that. I know of any number of cases where some of the best men I know anything about have been harassed, have been framed, and carted out almost overnight. They were men of very, very high type, unimpeachable character, who were blackmailed. The first step was to frame them in a manner so that there was no

Cobb: easy explanation. The next step was suspension. So rather than have a full investigation and have the matter go out in public and ruin them from here to kingdom come, they resigned. I knew a preacher that did that

Baum: I guess Mr. Camp was lucky that he wasn't in town.

Cobb: No. He wasn't in town at all, and I was there where he was supposed to have been, and could prove it. The case was dropped with no damage to Bill

Camp: Maybe they mistook me for you.

Cobb: Well, they misplaced the charge [Laughter] But you know, that is the most dastardly type of attack. It'll break your home up.

Camp: There is another thing in connection with that. There was a girl from Arkansas [I've forgotten her name] in charge of letter writing, and so on, who was with an assistant to Charlie Pratt. She came and told me what was going on; she'd heard it. She was the head of visé division, of all the letter writing. And this man was recognized in the government as the best composer of letters of all the officials in Washington. They had a visé outfit set up and they ruled out all the letters I dictated--hundreds of them--for the first few weeks.

Baum: Not well composed, was that the trouble?

Camp: I used the wrong kind of language. I used "yes" and "no."

They said, "You can't send those."

I said, "Who says I can't?"

Camp: "Well, they won't let you."

I said, "That's my type, and if they don't like it, it's just too bad."

This is something that didn't get to him until months later, I presume I didn't care. But this little lady came in and said, "I want to tell you about it But this I want you to know all of us know that you wouldn't have picked on this one if you'd have been interested at all." [Laughter]

She said, "You've got better taste than that "

Baum: You must have had fun around your office, with some good friends there, too.

Camp: All of the folks there were our friends, except the planted ones, all of them. And there were thousands of them, too. That's why he and I went through Hell and were able to win a battle. We didn't lose the war, either. But had it not been for this man, (Cobb), history would have been a lot different. They had their plan with all of this monkey business The communists had their plan: Negroes against whites, share-croppers against landlords, and so on. They're doing it today: Martin Luther King and the others are putting into effect the plan they had back then. Am I correct?

Cobb: Absolutely. I hope you realize we know what we're talking about

Baum: Both of you had the same experiences there.

Cobb: But isn't it hard to believe that human beings could stoop so low, depart so far from anything that could be judged right?

Camp: There are a lot of people in the world who don't appear to be interested in the human being, except to twist him to their philosophy. We just didn't belong to that tribe

Baum: I'm certainly grateful that we're getting this down in the record.

Cobb: I think it's all right to have a record like this because somewhere down the line it may guide somebody

Baum: It's essential to get it in the record, because otherwise, if only half the story is in the record, that's the half that's going to go down as history

Camp: Right Most of the people who set out to do a book or report were doing it to get in writing a document that would convey their own mean ideas to the world and posterity They weren't trying to get any facts. I read just a page or two there and ran right onto that the first thing

Baum: But if the facts exist, then they will refute them. When you go to a historical meeting, if you read something in a paper, there's going to be somebody sitting in the audience who's read the rest of the records.

Cobb: All of the statements that Mr. Camp and I have just made about how these people were fired can be documented by the press reports in all of the daily papers of the country, and particularly

Cobb: in Washington. They had headlines on it.

Camp: And it says just a few of them were fired And he said he wanted to fire Hiss. Hiss had already been put over in the State Department by Mrs. Roosevelt by that time. As I recall it, I may be a little off, he left the Cotton Division sometime early in '34.

Cobb: I think probably after we had completed development of the '34 program.

Camp: '34-'35 program.

Cobb: '34-'35 program. I think that's right, because I know there was a period there when he (Alger Hiss) and I sat across the table nearly all night long working on the details of the Program. But I happened to know the cotton situation and the cotton industry and he didn't; that was the only way in the world I ever won Plus the fact that we had these people in Congress who knew us and would go along.

Paragraph 7--Tenant Provisions

Baum: Well, let's go back for the record and discuss this purge of the AAA. The problem was the interpretation of Paragraph 7, on the landlord-tenant relations, wasn't it?

Cobb: Yes. And the interpretation was to the effect that you had to

Cobb: not only keep the same number of tenants but you had to keep the same identical tenants And our reaction was that this violates a basic law of business It says that you cannot make a private contract We were ready to take it to the Supreme Court or anyplace else. That would deny us the right of private contract, which you can't do under anybody's law anywhere. The Cotton Belt just went through the roof. And before you knew it, Congress was on its ear. Bill can tell you better what followed immediately, because I was in Texas at a meeting in Fort Worth. He called me about it. But he was present, and I'd rather have Bill tell you than tell you myself, because he was there while it was happening.

Baum: He's told me. You were in...?

Cobb: I was in a meeting in Fort Worth, Texas when this happened. What did happen was that congressmen and senators from the Cotton Belt went to Wallace to get him to fire the people who were responsible for this telegram. Paul Appleby wrote it. He was secretary to Secretary Wallace

Baum: Wasn't Wallace gone when that telegram was delivered?

Cobb: I'm not sure whether he was or not. I was out, and I wouldn't know. But he sent that telegram out

Baum: This was the telegram that said that Paragraph 7 must be interpreted that you must keep the same number and the identical tenants. And the Cotton Section had been interpreting it as

Baum: just the same number of tenants, more or less.

Cobb: Right. Now, we were responsible for that. The Cotton Section itself was responsible for putting in the statement that they keep the same number of tenants Because we just couldn't see the fairness of ejecting a whole group of people, putting them out of their homes, as any other provision would do They had something of a vested interest because they'd been there all these years. And we recognized that vested interest and said, "Now, listen, we are not going to be responsible for or a party to putting all these people out on the highway We will say that they must keep the same number, but suppose a tenant and his landlord had a violent quarrel and the landlord or the tenant had threatened to shoot the other one. Do you think we could force them to stay on the same farm together?" That's what they were saying: that they had to do that, denying the landlord the right of private agreement That was the sole basis of it. It didn't have a thing in the world to do with fairness, because they were going to keep them anyway unless they had some violent disagreement that made it impossible for them to work together.

That telegram was followed by a visit of congressmen and senators to Secretary Wallace's office. They said, "The people who are responsible for this telegram, for this interpretation, have got to be dismissed." Secretary Wallace didn't hear that

Cobb: to begin with He didn't follow through, so immediately--I think it was the next day--they went to the President. The next day, after they had presented the thing to the President, the President called Secretary Wallace and said, "These people have got to go "

What they had told the President was this: "Not one single penny of appropriation will be agreed to until this is done Those people have got to be put out of the federal government " That was two days later.

Camp: Now let me go back and reinforce this that Chester Davis said he didn't do. Early Monday morning, Cully was in Texas with wires and telephone calls coming in, raising cain. I called him quickly. We talked to tell him what was happening. E. D. White, in charge of the Cotton Program in Arkansas, happened to be there

I said, "Let's go upstairs to Tolley " We went quickly upstairs. We went in and Tolley said, "What's the matter, Bill"

I said, "The Cotton Program is going to bust up today "

He said, "What are you talking about?"

I said, "We're going to have it bust up. It's all through "

He looked and turned red,and said, "Well, well, well."

After a little talk he said, "Let's go down to see Chester Davis."

Camp: We went down the hall to see Chester Davis. We walked in, and Chester Davis was in trouble, but he didn't talk about that.

Chester said, "What do you want, Tolley?"

"Bill is on the warpath again."

Chester said, "What's the matter, Bill?"

I said, "There's nothing the matter with me. It's out in the country. And the Cotton Program is going to be busted up today. No more Cotton Program unless action is taken."

I told them that Cully Cobb was out of the office, in Texas, and I had talked to him, and this was understood a long time ago anyhow, that this was what was going to happen. Because they had tried to force it on us before.

Baum: The same interpretation?

Cobb: Yes. He had appointed a man and they had appointed a woman and there was a third one. There was a committee that worked on it for weeks and weeks, just that thing. Nothing else but that.

Baum: On the interpretation of that paragraph, or the writing of the paragraph?

Cobb: The writing of the paragraph, not the interpretation. Because we made it too clear to lend any other interpretation.

Camp: You are talking about two different things. The writing of it was in '34. But the interpretation, which you had already authorized the writing of, was in '35; it was a year old. We had already operated under it one year.

Cobb: They re-interpreted it and were looking for a chance to force it in, and they figured this was it. A main objective was to force Bill and me out of the government. It was to be the first step in taking away our administrative authority [Conrad's book].

Baum: There is a statement in here about Jerome Frank and the problem that came up with Norcross in Arkansas. Was this woman that worked on it Margaret Bennett?

Camp: She was a waspish little lawyer in Jerome Frank's office.

Cobb: I didn't know her, except when I saw her.

Baum: I notice that in this book a lot of people aren't mentioned that I know were there, which I think indicates that this man didn't consult all the sources that were available.

Camp: Jack Hudson isn't mentioned. Paul Porter isn't mentioned; Paul Porter became chairman of the National Democratic Committee, and he and Abe Fortas are law partners even now.

Cobb: Abe Fortas is a Supreme Court Justice. You're right. Then there was John Abt and Lee Pressman, and Jerome Frank, and Alger Hiss--our attorneys.

Camp: And Alger Hiss.

Cobb: Alger Hiss came in a little bit later, chronologically. He was there in spirit all the time.

Camp: Alger Hiss was with you all through '33 and the first months of '34.

Cobb: Oh yes.

Baum: Now here, Norcross wrote pointing out that he had more tenants in '34 than he'd had in '33, but not the same tenants. And it says here: "When Norcross's letter reached the desk of Jerome Frank, it caused a major explosion. For it was from reading the letter that Frank first learned that the Cotton Section was telling landlords they did not have to maintain the same tenants, only the same number." Do you suppose it's possible that Jerome Frank thought that all along the Cotton Section was telling the people they'd have to keep identical tenants?

Cobb: I can't believe it. We'd been in operation a year.

Baum: And you say this problem had already come up a number of times, about either the same number or the identical tenants?

Cobb: It came up when we wrote the original clause a year previously. We wouldn't agree to it, but we agreed to the other because it was quite proper in our judgment. From a humanitarian point of view, there was just no argument against it. Deny a man the right of private contract? Not and keep our form of government.

Camp: I've got telephone calls to make. I'll see you folks later. [Mr. Camp leaves.]

Baum: As far as you're concerned, it was perfectly clear that the Cotton Section and all the people out in the field were interpreting that it was the same number but not necessarily the same tenants, and that everyone knew that.

Cobb: There couldn't be any other interpretation. There were no if's nor and's about it. The clause was perfectly clear that they had to keep the same number of tenants, but not the same identical tenants. They all understood that. I didn't know of this particular case at all. It may have happened. If so, it's new to me. Probably did, just that way. Paul Appleby sent out the telegram.

Baum: Yes. It says Frank took the message to Wallace. No, [reading] "Chester Davis was out of town, so Jerome Frank notified assistant administrator Byrd that the Cotton Section had apparently been making legal opinions, and that his opinion section was preparing a new interpretation of Paragraph 7." I think that was what this all blew up about. I guess Chester Davis must have been out of town, and you were out of town.

Cobb: I was out of town. I was in Fort Worth, Texas, holding a meeting. They called me and I was presiding at that moment. I excused myself to go talk to Bill Camp about it.

Howard R. Tolley

Baum: Howard Tolley is not mentioned in this book at all.

Cobb: He was one of the prime movers in the beginnings, in the set-up that they had in mind for the agriculture of the entire nation:

Cobb: a complete bureaucracy, with everything channeled into and out of Washington, with Washington exercising all of the prerogatives, including appointment of everybody, fixing of salaries, fixing of working conditions, rules, regulations. Everything out of Washington Completely regimented agriculture. He was a party to that.

Baum. Did he have anything to do with the Cotton Section? Did you ever have to report to Tolley?

Cobb. Oh yes He was chief economist for the Department of Agriculture for years before this happened. [Formerly chief of the Division of Farm Management and Costs of the Bureau of Agricultural Economics] He had some authority to clear programs; I don't know what his authority was, at the moment

Baum: But Chester Davis .

Cobb. He was the administrator He was the man we reported to. Nobody else. He was the man we reported to, after Peek. Now, Peek was there to begin with, you remember.

Baum: Peek was there until he resigned in December, '33.

Cobb: Yes. And we reported to him up to that time But after that we reported to Chester Davis. And then Chester Davis, on up. But Tolley was in the Program Planning Division It probably would be proper to say that he was chairman of a planning committee They wouldn't call it that in official language, but that is probably a proper designation of his position and

Cobb his responsibility. chief of planning. And you can see what a strategic place that was. He was right in with all this other group that were working on this over-all program Comprehensive to the nth degree. Complete regimentation.

Chester C. Davis

Baum: It is not clear to me what position Chester Davis took on all this.

Cobb: Chester was sort of a middle-man. You never could quite find Chester. He was the type of person whose position you never knew too much about For that reason I could never imagine him doing what this man said he did

Baum: To dismiss all these

Cobb: Yes.

Baum: This Conrad book seems to imply that Chester Davis got them fired, that he got Wallace to agree to fire them

Cobb: The only thing that he ever wanted to do about firing anybody was when he came to me and said, "You've got to fire Bill Camp." And I said, "Ok. Start with me." That's the last I heard of that. It was months and months, maybe a year or two, before I told Bill about it. No point in bothering. Chester Davis is still living, he can verify that. I don't think he would tell

Cobb: about this case. But anyhow, that's it These personal incidents make a story quite readable and they are of enormous historic value, showing how governments operate even in a democracy.

Baum: Was there any difference in getting along with the administrator, getting along with George Peek, or getting along with Chester Davis?

Cobb: I never had enough relationship with George Peek to know about getting along with him. I got along all right with Chester Davis, because we understood each other completely. And where you have an understanding like that, why, everything works out all right.

Baum: Did Chester Davis try to stop any of the things you were trying to do?

Cobb: Not so far as I know. If he did, I was not aware of it.

Baum: You think he pretty much left you in charge of your part?

Cobb: I think he pretty much left us to our own devices. If I went back and got all the memorandums that passed between us, I might find something that I could pin some other type statement on. But so far as I know right now, we got along fine I was perfectly frank with him And he always knew--there never was any question as to what Bill was going to do and never any question as to what I was going to do. There never was any question in his mind about whether I was going to do what I

Cobb: told him I was going to do, either. That makes a wonderful basis for co-operation between two people, whether they think alike or see alike or not. So we got along. But he pretty much left us to our own devices. I realized the pressure he was under, and made allowances for that fact.

Friends in Congress

Baum: Apparently you had direct contact with congressmen and senators. Was that objected to, that somebody in the Department would go directly?

Cobb: No, and as far as I know there was no objection. I never heard of any objection. I don't know if they knew of all the contacts I had, because I didn't go around talking about it. I, of course, was asked to help with legislation. But Congressman W. J. Driver had come to me long before this thing [the purge] had happened--he was from Arkansas--and said, "These people have got to go." He was chairman of the House Appropriations Committee. He had been in my office a number of times. A wonderful gentleman. Of course, I knew our own senators from Georgia. Senator Bankhead and Senator Smith were on the agricultural committees. Pat Harrison was from Mississippi and I had known him long before he became a United States senator.

Baum: You'd known him when you worked in Mississippi?

Cobb: Yes, I knew him when I worked down in Mississippi. And of course, I knew Senator Robinson from Arkansas, Joe Robinson. Today, they'd tell you exactly what happened. I kept them fully informed.

Baum. You knew them as an agricultural writer?

Cobb: I knew them as an agricultural writer to begin with. And they knew me long before I ever went to Washington. I kept them completely informed. Nobody could slip up on the blind side. And Dick Kleberg (Richard Mifflin Kleberg)--by the way, President Johnson was his secretary--was chairman of the Agricultural Committee in the House, at the time. He lived in Corpus Christi, Texas; and his wife was one of these King Ranch daughters. I've been in their home, and I knew them very, very well, indeed. They'd had a lot of trouble there with their cotton, in the territory around the Robbstown area. I had been there with some entomologists, they had a disease there that they were tremendously worried about. I visited Dick Kleberg way back there and I knew him all along. I'd been on the King Ranch when he was there. So I knew these people.

Baum: I wonder if some of your friends, in the Senate for instance, insisted on your appointment to your position.

Cobb: So far as I know, no. If one of them even made a suggestion, I don't know it. They may have. I figured it was of Wallace's

own choosing I don't know of anything to the contrary. I know he did clear it with Senator Russell, I guess because I was from Georgia

That's just polite for patronage

That's it Just polite, that's all. I hadn't been there two days before I went over and talked to Senator Russell, and he told me what it was they'd done But so far as I know, it was all out of a clear sky I was then managing editor of the Progressive Farmer in Birmingham. We had sold the Southern Ruralist to the Progressive Farmer, and I went with the sale to Birmingham as managing editor of the Progressive Farmer. I was at my desk working when the call came from Secretary Wallace. I said, "Well, just give me a few minutes to clear it with some people here and I'll tell you what's what." I turned around and called them back and I said, "Ok, I'll be there tomorrow." That was it

You'd just lost your wife about then, hadn't you? [Cully Cobb married Byrdie Ball in 1910. She died in 1932.]*

Yes. Just about that time.

So that brought you to Washington alone.

That brought me to Washington alone.

And you had two boys to take care of?

That's right. I had two boys. And they were in the best of hands back in Atlanta. I had a home in Atlanta, and I had a

*In August, 1934, Mr. Cobb married Lois P Dowdle of Atlanta, Georgia. (See page 105 et seq.)

Cobb: housekeeper that knew the children and loved them. She took care of that situation until we could get it straightened out.

Baum: After the February, 1935, purge, did things go easier in the Cotton Division, or was there still harassment?

Cobb: There was a period of time there when the quietness was alarming. There wasn't a rumble, no sound of distant thunder. [Laughter]

Baum: Must have been a little dull.

Cobb: It was quite dull. That storm had blown over. We weren't bothered too much. Of course you had it all the time, because they (the communists) were building, infiltrating all the time, out in the back country. They don't stop that. It goes on all the time; it's going on now, just as it's going on in the San Joaquin Valley, organizing the tenants, for whom they care nothing, and that sort of stuff. The hunt for pawns goes on all the time. But we had a period there of alarming quiet. We were worried about what wasn't going on. Maybe something was. The "Great Revolution" is still to be realized, however.

Baum: Maybe that's what Chester Davis meant when he said, "I haven't heard about you for a whole week."

Cobb: He said, "Cobb, what's going wrong? They haven't made a drive on you this whole week."

Efforts to Pass a One-Variety Cotton Enabling Act

Baum: Mr Camp said that at one point it seemed like you would be able to get in an enabling act for one-variety cotton

Cobb: Yes. You had better work that out with him. I can give you the bare details He had been responsible for the one-variety cotton program here in California We had developed a program completely, including the manner in which it was to be financed. We had it up to the point of announcement: that in each state [or a region if it could be regional] the state director of the experiment station and the state director of the experiment station in another state would be allowed to agree on one variety of cotton, where growing conditions [including soil and water and all] were similar. It was just ready to go to the field; and the Secretary had tentatively agreed to it, when one day he came in right out of the clear and told us that they couldn't go through with it.

The Coker Seed Company in South Carolina is a cottonseed producer, and it opposed it As it came to me, they had gotten hold of Secretary Wallace. Old man Dave Coker was a cottonseed breeder [a plant breeder, not only cottonseed, but cotton essentially] and Wallace was a corn breeder. And they had been associated in the past years. Coker regarded this as a very grave threat to the production and sale of cottonseed, and he was a big producer and a big seller of purebred cottonseed. As I have the story, he went to Wallace and told him

Cobb: what it would do to his program of intensive breeding and sales. And it was on the strength of that that Wallace called the program off.

If we could have gone through with that, there just isn't any telling how many millions of dollars that would have added to the value of cotton lint through the years since that time, to the producers of this country.

That's one of the sad stories in connection with this. I think probably just about the saddest It doesn't make any difference what comes or goes of anybody's Cotton Program. Anything that helps to produce better quality and more pounds of that better quality is essential, whatever your program is To me that has been one of the saddest facts of our whole program. And we had it so we could put it in effect in not more than two years. They would have to decide definitely on the variety that they were going to recommend as the one variety for their region. Then they were going to have to be sure that they could get seed In some cases it would require the production of seed of a selected variety. That would mean the production of seed this year for next year's planting. So in two years we could have had the entire Cotton Belt growing the one variety in every region that was best suited to that region's natural and artificial conditions Now there's no telling what the increase in economic output in actual dollars

Cobb: and cents would have been. Bill and I were just floored.

Baum: Mr. Camp said something about South Carolina director of Extension D. W. Watkins opposing it.

Cobb: Yes, he opposed it. He was in South Carolina, and you can understand the relationship between the director and the Coker Seed Company. And then, D. W. just didn't see it I don't think he was opposed to it for the same reason that the Cokers would have been. He just couldn't see its value as Bill and I could see it, and he was opposed to it.

Baum: I suppose a lot of these Extension men were opposed to what would look like more government regulation.

Cobb: Most of them were And that might have been in the back of his head. I don't know what his whole reason was. And if the Secretary called him, I think he would have agreed with the Secretary that the best thing to do was just abandon the thing. But he's been sorry ever since, that he did do that

Baum: He's seen the value of it since, is that right?

Cobb: He's seen the value of it, and has remarked more than once what it is doing for this community and that community, and some other, in his own state. Undoubtedly he has demeaned himself down through the years for the fact that he didn't go along back there.

Baum: Was that one of the points you promoted in your magazine?

Cobb: One variety?

Baum: One variety, yes.

Cobb: Oh yes Yes, I had been doing that for a long time. One regional variety for all crops.

Baum: It certainly has been wonderful here in California.

Cobb: It would be wonderful every place else. There's no reason why it wouldn't be just as good for any other territory where cotton is produced as it would be here. Because more pounds of quality cotton per acre was our goal, the words should always be coupled together

Relations With the Press and Public

Cobb: When I got off the train in Washington in 1933, when I went up there to answer Henry Wallace's call, the representative of one of the news services, the Associated Press, met me at the train and wanted to know if I was I, and I told him I was. [Laughter] And where I had come from, and I told him that. And what I was going to do, and I told him that this was what I was going to look into. And he said, "Now, what would your objective be?" They know how to ask leading questions.

I said, "I've got just exactly one objective," and he got his pencil out. And I answered him with these words: "I am going to do all I can to make agriculture a paying

Cobb: business "

He said, "Where, where "

I said, "That's all I've got to say now We'll work in the details later. Are you here in Washington?"

He said, "Yes, I'm here in Washington."

I said, "Come to see me later on, and I'll give you all the details That, now, is the only objective I have to make agriculture in the South a paying business "

He said, "It's not a paying business now."

I said, "Are you asking me?"

And he came to see me after that. He was a pretty frequent visitor. He came to my office day after day and week after week the whole time that I was in Washington

Among those others who came to my office so many times was Felix Bel Air, of the New York Times. Felix was a perfectly wonderful person; I believe he's still with the New York Times. They used to go over to our house. We lived in Arlington, Virginia.

Every Thanksgiving we gave the newspaper representatives a Thanksgiving dinner We had a big table with country ham and lye hominy and hot biscuits and red eye gravy and coffee We had a small house, but it had a chimney with a fireplace, and we could accomodate twenty-five or thirty people in the living room if they sat on the floor. Well, they came in

Cobb: there, the living room, after we had finished our dinner--and you can eat 'till you pop if you have lye hominy to go along with ham, and it'd never hurt you And they'd eat 'till they'd pop. Then we'd go into the living room and sit down. A lot of them would sit down on the floor, flat on the floor, and just take their hair down. I was a newspaperman; now, if you think a newspaperman will violate a confidence between him and somebody else--he's just not going to do it That's one thing he will not do. So, every Thanksgiving, I had opportunity, as in between times, to check up on what they knew; and they didn't fail to tell it, exactly like it was--who, what, and when. There was never any doubt about that. And I had that advantage, that probably nobody else in Washington did have.

This is the thing I was going to tell you. Mrs. Cobb and I are both teetotalers, always have been. One Thanksgiving after we had finished one of these sumptuous meals, Felix had been sitting down right in front of the fire. And before getting up to go, he got up off of the floor and said, "I want to make a statement,right here and now I want to thank the Cobbs for the fact that they don't feel like they've got to make us drunk to make us have a good time. And how many of y'all feel that way?"

And they all said, "Amen." Wasn't that wonderful?

: So it was an advantage to you to be a teetotaler?

: Absolutely. It was a reflection of respect. It was just one of the most refreshing experiences I've ever had. And Felix was just one of the smartest boys you've ever met in your life. They all were. Those people have to be smart. And they were. And they were good. You find one now and then that's not exactly what he ought to be, but he doesn't last; they've got to be good people. As far as I'm concerned, I can trust them when I have a little doubt, maybe, about somebody else.

But we did that every year when we were there, and it was one of the things we always looked forward to. And I've had them ask me long before Thanksgiving, "Are we going to have our dinner?" They never would let anything else interfere with that red gravy dinner at the Cobbs' on Thanksgiving. We enjoyed it, of course. It was very, very wonderful.

: I've read of areas where the Cotton Program was not well received.

: Oh yes, there were people who didn't like it. Norman Thomas, while not one of the most offensive, did what he could to make trouble for me.

: He helped with the Southern Tenant Farmers...

: Southern Tenant Farmers Union. Yes, and here's what they did to him. He came over there to address a Southern Tenant Farmers Union gathering. I think it probably was at Tyronza, where

Cobb: Mitchell lived. And when they had all gotten in the schoolhouse hall, the sheriff went in, arrested him, and took him to Memphis, and I don't think he's been back since.

I don't know about Bill, but I've been threatened more than one time. I was threatened one time that if I came to fill an engagement I had in Blytheville, in northeast Arkansas, I would be shot. That is in that same Tenant Farmers Union territory, you know, and they had worked up a good deal of sentiment there in the Blytheville area that was antagonistic. One of the most fortunate things in the world was that, when I got up on the platform to address the group, one of the men in the very front of the audience, was an ex-county agent, a Negro, who had been a county agent back in Mississippi when I was there as an Extension worker. He was sitting right in front of me. And as I saw him we recognized each other and I knew, of course, what the feeling was--you could feel it in the air, a thing like that. I called him by name and said, "What in the world are you doing in Arkansas?"

He said, "Well, Mr. Cobb, am I glad to see you."

I said, "What are you doing here?"

He said, "Farming." (I knew about it.)

I said, "You own your own land?"

He said, "Yes, sir. I own my own land."

And I asked him how much. I think it was half a section,

Cobb: maybe a section of that rich delta soil.

And I said, "Getting along all right?"

He said, "I got it paid for."

I said, "You're doing all right. Who are your neighbors?"

Well, one of them was one of our district managers in that territory.

He said, "He is my neighbor."

I said, "You all get along all right?"

He said, "He gets in the grass, and I help him out. And when I get in the grass, he helps me out."

We talked for a little while, and then I made the statement that I came there to make. But after I had finished that dialogue with that Negro--he was just as fine a person as you ever saw in your life, very, very able (he'd been a good county agent, and I knew it)--the shooting was over. You've never seen such a change take place in an audience. It took place two seconds after I spoke to him.

He said, "I've got my farm paid for."

I said, "Stand up, I want these people here to see one man in the Delta who owns his own land." And they all clapped their hands.

As far as I was concerned about the success of the meeting, it was over. You don't find things like that every day, but somehow they do happen. I wonder if it was a coincidence.

Cobb: Whether it was or not, he was at the right place at the right time (for the sake of our program) and I was too. Then we went on and had a wonderful meeting after that. When I'd finished with what I had to say, we threw the meeting open to questions and had an old-fashioned get-together. After that, I don't believe any threat was made on us. So far as I know, there wasn't. But I'd been told to keep out.

Baum: It took quite a bit of courage to go there.

Cobb: Not too much. You just know it's not so.

Mrs. Lois Dowdle Cobb, Home Economist, and the Promotion of Oleomargarine

Baum: When I came in and you introduced me to Mrs. Cobb, you said she had been on the staff of the home economics division of the University of Georgia. [Mr. Cobb was married to Lois P. Dowdle of Atlanta, Georgia, on August 24, 1934.]

Cobb: Yes. She was with the University of Georgia, in the Home Economics division. She had started out as a schoolteacher. She had come all the way up from county agent, district agent, on up to the very top. She was a graduate of the University of Georgia, and had studied at Cornell too.

Baum: You said she had been active in promoting the use of oleomargarine.

Cobb: Yes. After she had changed her work. She had been editor of the home division of the Southern Ruralist, and she went with the Progressive Farmer at the same time I did. They wanted somebody to take over the promotional work for the Oleomargarine Institute, and she was the person that they selected to do that. And she did a whale of a job getting it accepted. She had headquarters in Washington when we were married

Baum: Getting oleomargarine socially accepted, or legally accepted? Or both?

Cobb: Legal acceptance of course, was the first hurdle. And it isn't socially accepted yet, not wholeheartedly You don't look on oleomargarine as you would on butter. I think there is still that feeling. I don't think you would so much any more.

Baum: It is used regularly for certain purposes

Cobb: Oh, for certain uses, yes. You never think about using anything else. For cakes and other baking and cooking purposes, margarine costs much less than butter and gives the same results But socially, I think you still find some little resistance.

Baum: But her job was legal acceptance.

Cobb: Her job was to get legal acceptance. That was what her job was. She worked with the home economic divisions of the

Cobb: universities from one end of the country to the other. And for the most part they were in sympathy completely with what she was doing, because you could buy oleomargarine that you couldn't tell from butter to save your life, for about one third the price of butter One of the funniest things that you ever saw happened at the Toll Gate Inn, out from Washington; it was a famous eating place. The margarine industry had called a meeting of leading chemists of the fats and oil manufacturers, and Mrs. Cobb was to have a test to see if anybody could tell margarine from butter. After the thing was over, they asked questions to find out who could tell which was what I don't remember now if they failed to bring the margarine or the butter, one or the other. They failed to bring the two samples. They had any number of people say they could tell the difference, this was butter and this was margarine. [Laughter] It was all one. Well, you've never seen such a flabbergasted crowd in your life as when they found out it was all either butter or margarine, I don't remember which now. They felt sure that somebody had pulled a trick on them, but they hadn't I think they all went away believing that they'd been swindled But there they were: "Oh yes, this is butter," "This is the difference, now. Let me show you how it spreads."

Baum. How long did Mrs. Cobb work on that?

Cobb: Oh, I don't know. Two or three years. Something like that.

Baum: Was that in the thirties that she was working on that?

Cobb: Yes, that was back in the thirties.

Attempt of Franklin D. Roosevelt to Purge Senator George

Baum: Also, you were going to tell me what happened when Franklin Roosevelt was trying to purge Senator George.

Cobb: He and Senator George had had a violent disagreement.

In his determined attempt to pack the Supreme Court of the United States, President Roosevelt found Senator Walter F. George, senior senator from Georgia to be his most vigorous, most determined, and most effective opponent. In many other extreme cases, most of them left-wing in character, Senator George used his tremendous influence in the United States Senate in opposition to many of the President's various and sundry plans to reshape the government of the United States to his liberal liking. But it was Senator George's unyielding opposition to packing the Supreme Court that embittered President Roosevelt and caused him to decide that if he was to have his way he would have to get rid of the senator.

On March 11, 1938, at a huge regional meeting at

Cobb: Barnesville, Georgia, for which the President had long prepared, the President felt that the time was right and that the day of purge was at hand Senator George, a number of state dignitaries, and many of President Roosevelt's Washington inner circle were on the speaker's stand with him.

In his suave and polished manner, the President proceeded to move toward that portion of his speech in which he told the audience in the most vindictive and vitriolic terms what he thought of Senator George and urged them to vote for Lawrence Camp, who was then running against Senator George for the Senate seat that Senator George had held for some sixteen years Here is some of the language [in quotes] the President used. The quotes are taken from the report of Felix Belair of the New York Times, as they appeared in the August 1, 1938, issue of the Times:

After saying that the Senator was "a dyed-in-the-wool conservative," President Roosevelt proceeded to compare the senator to a number of Republicans he did not like and branded Senator George as "a representative of the corporate dictatorship which has enslaved millions of our people for more than half a century." And then this. "Therefore, answering the request from many citizens of Georgia that I make my position clear, I have no hesitation in saying that if I were able to vote in the September primaries in this state, I most assuredly

Cobb: would cast my ballot for Lawrence Camp." There was much more in the President's statement that was not only insulting to Senator George but was quite as insulting to his hearers However, Senator George knew what the President was going to say and was prepared to meet the attack with a reply that let the President know how he felt and that the battle was on Here is Senator George's answer:

"Mr President, I regret that you have taken this occasion to question my democracy and attack my public record. I want you to know I accept the challenge." This marked the beginning of the precipitous decline of Roosevelt's popularity.

Some time before the Barnesville speech, Sam Bledsoe, who was in the Information Division of the U. S. Department of Agriculture, handed me a slip of paper with the foregoing quotes from the President's speech on it and told me that these statements had been taken from the final draft of the speech the President was going to make at Barnesville and that he thought I would be interested in them. A few days later I gave the slip of paper to Senator George in his headquarters in the Henry Grady Hotel in Atlanta, Georgia. The Senator's reaction at first was one of shock and complete disbelief. He stated that no person of high place, let alone the President of the United States, could possibly stoop so low as to do such a dastardly thing. He said it just could

Cobb: not be so. And that while he believed me, he felt that I had gotten the wrong information.

I said to him, "Senator George, whatever may be your belief, the statements on that slip of paper were taken from the final draft of the speech President Roosevelt is going to make at Barnesville on August 11. And it would be my suggestion that you accept them as they are written and prepare your answer."

Some weeks after the election was over, and Senator George had been overwhelmingly returned to his seat in the Senate of the United States, I was called to his suite in the Henry Grady Hotel. He met me at the door and his first remark was, "I still don't believe it."

After we were seated, he continued: "Had I not had that slip of paper with its unbelievable statements, I would not only have been totally unprepared, but I am sure I would have been so shaken and so amazed that I would scarcely have known what to do."

"Even so," he said, "almost immediately the President started his speech, I <u>saw it coming</u>, and finally he repeated the words on that slip of paper that I had kept so carefully tucked away in my pocket. And now I want to thank you from the bottom of my heart for just about the greatest kindness that anybody could possibly show a friend. It is completely

Cobb: without precedent, and I am still kicking myself for my first reaction of disbelief. And I think I will have to trust you from here on out "

More on the Press

Baum: And you also had friends in the newspaper world.

Cobb: Oh, I had friends in the newspaper world. I knew them all. Felix Belair, of the New York Times, was among them. I knew Drew Pearson, knew him very well. And Drew came over quite frequently to begin with. Some case came up in Mississippi, I don't remember what it was, but it was supposed to be a violent clash between a landlord and his tenants, or something to that effect Drew came over and wanted to know about it.

I said, "Well now, Drew, the best thing is not for me to sit here and talk to you. But I'll just give you the file on the whole thing, and you can check that against the questions that you were going to ask me." He took the file and he fingered it a little bit, and that didn't satisfy him.

I said, "I haven't got a thing under the sun to tell you. It's all right there in the file, right before you. You read the file and you get your facts out of the file. Then what you say will be the truth "

Cobb: I did that to him two or three times, and he hasn't been back to see me since. His little brother used to come over quite frequently, but Drew let me alone. Give him the file, it will have all the facts that he wants. And that's the way that we followed up our work. In any case of that kind that came to us, we went in right that minute to get the facts ourselves. If anybody wanted them, they got the file. But these other men, they would come for legitimate purposes. That's the only case that I know of where I was sure that the purpose was not legitimate from a newspaper standpoint

Baum: What do you think Drew Pearson wanted?

Cobb: He wanted some sensationalism, I think. He was always hunting sensationalism, and he probably thought he would find something that would reflect on me, and he'd have a big story, or reflect on the Southern Cótton Division, that would provide a big story. I don't know what his reason was. I don't believe anybody could tell you, except that yòu would know that it was going to be sensational. That's what he dealt with. He let me alone because I'd give him the file and let him get his own figures. If you quote off the record, or away from the record, or make any statement, then he can say, "You said this." But I never gave him anything.

Baum: You never gave him any information, except the facts he could look at.

Cobb: Not a thing except, "Here are the facts, get your information from these facts." That was Bill's attitude, the attitude of the whole Division. We stayed out of the press except when these men like Felix Belair came to us for a legitimate story about a legitimate subject. We never had any troubles with the press. Not one single instance that I can remember. Because we were not evasive, we never tried to evade anything. If they did have something, some questions, we said, "All right, now, here are the facts. You're newspaperman enough to know what to do with them. Here they are." Newspaper people of standing are pretty fair, they are quite reasonable, when you accept them and respect them for what they think they are and really are; and they are, as a rule, completely objective and completely honest You'll find some that will try to work a political slant in on you. But as for me, I don't believe many would do that. They didn't to us, at any rate.

Baum: So you feel you were certainly treated fairly by the press.

Cobb: Personally, yes. Absolutely. And there was no abuse of any information I gave the press.

Baum: Do you think all the departments were? Or was it possibly because you were known to them as a newspaper man?

Cobb: The press that I had association with, not the press as a rule.

Baum: I'm talking about the press in the thirties, when you were

Baum: there.

Cobb: Well, we had these dirty stories all up and down the country, like this Memphis thing I was telling you about, in Time magazine. We had all of that. But I was talking about my own personal relationship with the representatives of the press. They never dealt unfairly with me, personally. But there were those who would fan up an instance like this Mamie Sue Blagden case. That was in Time. They were not my friends and Time was by no means my choice of magazines

Baum: Time magazine. That wasn't the Washington press.

Cobb: Oh no, that wasn't the Washington press. It was Time magazine It went out to get a sensational story. They found plenty of sources of sensational stories like that, and most of them just as groundless. Ninety-nine and nine-tenths per cent of them were just as groundless as "Mamie Sue Blagden." They had laid her over a log and had just beaten the tar out of her with a wide leather strap, according to her story. She probably had never been out of Memphis; I doubt if she ever had Anyway, nobody in the Memphis territory believed her story

Cobb: Those who seemed to know said the black marks were not bruises. It was paint or grease as was found out later What a frame-up.

Baum: It was just a fake picture--that is, the stripes were. The

Baum: balance was for real. In Time she was pictured as a girl who had been gravely mistreated.

Cobb: She was supposed to have been in the sharecropper section of Arkansas. So the story goes, she'd been over there on one of these escapades, organizing or sympathizing, or something. I don't know what they claimed she was doing over there. As a matter of fact, as indicated, I don't know whether she'd ever been in Arkansas. But she said she had, and she said they'd beaten her up with a razor strop

We had another case like that. We had a Presbyterian preacher who performed the funeral service for a Negro who was supposed to have been murdered. I called James P. Davis, our Negro field agent, who had headquarters in Little Rock, the minute that came out in the papers, and I said, "Jim, what about this boy that's been murdered down in Arkansas?" [Naming the place]

He said, "Mr. Cobb, you know nobody has been murdered down there."

I said, "I don't know whether they have or not. The paper says they have, and that a white Presbyterian minister, I believe his name is Williams, performed the funeral services."

He said, "Nobody's been murdered down there "

I said, Well, listen,Jim, if they haven't, we want to

Cobb: know it; and if they have, we want to know it."

He said, "Just give me time. I'll dig him up for you." [That's the exact language he used, and he was talking out of Little Rock.]

About two weeks later I had a telephone call from Jim, in Chicago. He said, "I got the problem solved sooner than I thought."

I said, "What is it, Jim?"

He said, "I dug up your nigger. He's here, and here's where he lives, in Chicago."

I said, "You mean you've seen him?"

He said, "Yes, sir, here he is."

I said, "I thought they buried him in Arkansas."

He said, "Well, they ain't buried him yet. He's right here, here in Chicago."

Well, the church put this preacher out right away He knew what he was doing, too

Baum: You mean there wasn't anybody buried there?

Cobb: No! There wasn't anybody buried, the whole thing was a frame-up, fiction. And Jim found the man they were supposed to have buried, alive, about ten days later. I don't know how he found out. But he found out from some of the Negroes in the territory that he had gone to Chicago, so he followed him and found him. They were doing that kind of thing all

Cobb: the time.

As Bill said, there isn't any length to which that type of publicity hound won't go in order to get a story or, in our case, to discredit a program. That was what that was intended to do. Of course, it got nationwide publicity. The fact that the Negro was found alive never got in the press. The sensational first story was out The other one never even got in the press. Nobody else could ever have "dug" that Negro up or used the words that Jim used, because I think that gives you the feeling of disgust and the color that you've got to have to understand him. Nobody could have found him except another Negro. If I should offer any documentary evidence as to whether or not we had gotten the right man in Jim Davis, I think this is it.

Baum: Is Jim Davis still alive?

Cobb: No, he is dead. He had a very fine woman for a wife They lived in Little Rock, Arkansas. I've been to see them. They had a daughter in Canada, I believe she was in Quebec. She married an Englishman. After his wife died, Jim didn't live too long. But he was one of the finest persons in this world, just as smart as he could be.

Comments on Land-Grant Colleges, Agricultural Extension, and Mississippi State University

Baum: You said there had been a lot of feeling in the southern area, opposing Extension in the land-grant colleges for a certain amount of time.

Cobb: It goes back to the very beginning of the land-grant colleges The universities rejected the land-grant colleges to begin with. I think there is no better example than in our own state of Mississippi. It was first to be located at the University of Mississippi, at Oxford. It was located there--the land-grant college. They had a farm and everything. But they could never even get any students, so they closed it up right quick Then it was relocated at Starkville, Mississippi That's over in the edge of the prairie belt. Now, like land-grant colleges everywhere, it is now one of the great universities of the whole country. Tremendous student body, and doing tremendous work.

Baum: What was the basis of the opposition?

Cobb: Because it was not classical or professional enough

Baum: It was too technical, it was too practical.

Cobb: It was too technical It was like the attitude of the territory of the area outside the South was toward our Agricultural Adjustment Program. The colleges did not want

Cobb: it at all to begin with. They said it was an action program with very objectionable regulatory features and they were engaged in a teaching or education program I could never quite understand what the real difference was. But they just didn't want to have anything to do with it at all to begin with, and would not have had, except they came to know that if they did not go along with what we were organizing, they would be by-passed entirely and that they would contribute to the almost immediate downfall of Extension work

Mr. Evans was probably the strongest individual we had at the time in relation to the colleges of agriculture and Extension work outside the South, because he could talk to them in their own language. He had been in it for many, many years. He'd sit down with the directors and say, "Either you're going to do this or you're through. You've got your choice. From my point of view, it is the perfectly proper thing for us to do in our territory It's the thing we want to do, it's the thing that will enhance our activities more than anything else that we could do It will bring into it forces that will help us to achieve objectives that we have been absolutely unable to approach with any assurance that we'd get there in any reasonable length of time. We're jumping over dozens and dozens of decades at a time in what we are doing here "

Baum: When you say "we," you mean Extension?

Cobb: As an Extension agent, he was talking about the Extension forces in the South and then Extension work as a whole. He said, "Because this is going to give a power back of our program that we haven't had before. The federal government in the program has only one objective, and that is "making agriculture a paying business." They can see that And that gives them [Extension workers] an approach to the farmers that we've never had to the same degree. Boy, we can go to town. And we are going to go to town, but we can't go unless you go too. We'll lose if you lose "

Baum: So, Evans' point was that for the Extension workers to join the AAA program would build up Extension.

Cobb: It would give them power that they had never had before. And it did.

Baum: Of course, your point of view was to get good men who were already out in the field and knew the territory, working on your program

Cobb: Men that knew the territory, knew the problems of the territory, knew the people of the territory as nobody else could, as only the pastor of a church can know his people. And they knew them in that same way and with that same type of relationship.

Baum: I know Mr. Crocheron out here in California objected to

Baum: using the Extension for AAA work.

Cobb: Oh yes. He was very much against it. We had to by-pass him. They gave us a lot of trouble with the county agents up and down the cotton territory. But we had Bill in Washington who knew this territory, and he knew the people. So it wasn't too much trouble to us I've been to the university here and talked to Mr Crocheron, and Mr. Tippett, and the balance of them We've had our meetings here. They didn't amount to too much because they were not at all enthusiastic about the program, not at all.

Baum: I think Crocheron didn't want the agents involved in anything that was regulatory.

Cobb: No. Nothing that was regulatory or had work in it.

Baum: I think he favored action programs, but only in helping the farmer as an outside person. But with no way to enforce anything.

Cobb: Nothing regulatory. And that would be a more appropriate term than "action." But it had "regulatory" in it, and he was bitterly opposed to that. It didn't make an awful lot of difference because we had the program well in hand anyway, so we went right on.

Baum: And it was the same thing during the war, when the county agents also did certain work for the government.

Cobb: They had to do it. But that was it. No "regulatory."

Cobb: Theirs was administrative, not regulatory

Baum: When you were in Mississippi working in Extension, was Extension a popular program with the farmers?

Cobb: Very popular. To begin with, it wasn't Because they had to be brought around to the point where they understood it It was not popular to begin with because they didn't understand it.

Baum: It was changing their methods of working?

Cobb: Yes Not violently It was a considered approach all the way through, nothing violent. The thing that helped most was the invasion of the boll weevil; that just about wiped out the cotton industry of the entire South for a period of time. They knew they had to have something to take its place. And they knew that they didn't know what to do, so they were quite willing to listen to the College of Agriculture and the Extension forces and the Experiment Stations. A calamity was what gave Extension work its open door to their minds, and to their hearts later on. They really came to know what Extension work could do and was doing.

Baum: And the land-grant colleges were not acceptable at first, is that right?

Cobb: No, not acceptable to the educational forces. But they were to the farmers. At the time, when our college in Mississippi was being brought into being, the Grange was then a moving

Cobb: spirit. And a great number of the better farmers in the state belonged to the Grange at that time. [Patrons of Husbandry was what they called them.] They were largely responsible for putting through the legislation that, in the first place, created the colleges of agriculture and accepted the land-grant provision. Having these members of the Grange, who were the outstanding citizens of every farming community in the state, promoting it, why, you were a long way ahead in introducing it to the farmers of the communities themselves You had these people pulling for you. And they fought for it in season and out.

Our first president down there was General Stephen D. Lee. He was a cousin of General Robert E. Lee. He had come back from the Civil War to a big cotton plantation in the prairie or Black Belt. Black in two ways: black land, the prairie; and the large number of tenants.

Baum: "Black Belt" refers to the soil, doesn't it?

Cobb: That's right. "Black Belt" in Mississippi refers to the soil. But in some territories they call the place where the Negroes live "Black Belt." These happen to be the same thing in this case. But General Stephen D. Lee was its first president. He was a graduate of West Point. When the War between the States was declared, he came back to the South and distinguished himself as a Confederate

Cobb: general. Like General Robert E. Lee. He felt obliged to come back to his people, and he did. And I have had the privilege of knowing every president of that college except one, from that time down to now. That was Governor Stone. After General Lee resigned, Governor Stone took over. He died within a period of about six months, I think He was followed by Dr. J. C. Hardy. And I was there under Dr. Hardy's regime. So I've known the history of the college from its beginnings up to this moment. That's not important, however, for the story about Bill Camp

Baum: Agricultural Extension is a large part of the story

Cobb: We have just erected a granite marker to General Stephen D. Lee. About the second year of his presidency, he worked out the details that he wanted carried out with reference to irrigation in the upland territory. And he ordered a pool built on the college campus. It was an organized research program that he was introducing, to find out how impounded water in the hill country of Mississippi could be used to grow vegetables, particularly, have vegetables available every month in the year, and then for other crops also. He had come from a plantation where the people, white and black, were always on short rations They had a garden for a little period in the springtime. When the hot summer came, they didn't have anything until the turnip patch,

Cobb: planted the middle of August, gave them turnip salad and a little bit later turnips and potatoes--sweet potatoes. But they were always on a very restricted ration. And he knew they would be until they could find some way to grow crops throughout the year, and they couldn't do it without water. So he ordered Professor A. B McKay, who was then professor of horticulture, to build this pool there on the campus and to pipe the water down to the truck-growing acreage First of all, to produce vegetables for the mess hall, and as a research program. Basically it was research, but at the same time it had the very practical view of producing vegetables for the mess hall for the boys. They had no supermarkets and there was no distribution of fruits and vegetables then as we now have them. The only thing we ever had there was the banana car that came up from Mobile once a month and parked on the campus to sell to the boys. That's about the only thing in exotic fruits and vegetables that we had. That was a very practical problem that he was setting this thing up to meet.

We are erecting a marker down there on the edge of the pool. It's up now and it will be dedicated next spring. I haven't told Bill, but he'll be at the dedication. It marks the first point in the history of agriculture, so

Cobb: far as the historian Dr. John Scott has been able to find, and he's searched the records from one end of the country to the other It marks the very beginnings of organized research to determine the value of impounded water in the rain belt for the production of fruits and vegetables and other crops. Tremendously significant.

General Stephen D. Lee was a graduate of West Point. No person could have had better training for the problems that he had than a person who had been trained like that I've thought about that a lot, and wondered why it wouldn't have been better if they had found a graduate of a college of agriculture [there wasn't any, as far as that goes], but long ago I decided in my own mind that he was the best possible trained man for it Because at West Point, he had to plan. He was disciplined in every way that a person can be disciplined. Before he could get anywhere, he had to study military science and tactics, and he had to reduce his plans to paper. And his plans had to have an objective before they could be approved by anybody in the faculty there, and that objective had to be worth fighting for. Now that's exactly what he did in this thing and in all of his work. He laid a foundation under that college that they have never been able to get away from, a foundation of down to earth practicality. Today it's one of the great

Cobb: institutions of the world because General Lee worked into it that solid approach that they haven't been able to get away from, that nobody has wanted to get away from. Well, now then, just the other day I was reading a report where they had doubled the production of milk because of a pool identical to this, the McKay pool, at the Holly Springs Experiment Station in north Mississippi

But one of the interesting things is this He, General Lee, ran into the same trouble at the beginning that I ran into when we sent our first boys from Mississippi to Chicago in 1918. I sent a group of boys, one from each congressional district John Swaim, who was in charge of Boys Club work in Oklahoma, sent a group too. I think we had eighteen all told. Before we sent them there, we had tried to work out a program with Dean C. F. Curtis, chairman of the agricultural committee of the International Livestock Show, that would provide the boys with a judging contest. He was bitterly opposed to it, and said very frankly that he did not want these children up there messing up their work. I never was able to work out anything with him at all, but with Barnie Hyde, who was secretary, I was able to work out a plan for the next year. That was the beginning of the International 4-H Club Congress at the International Livestock Show in Chicago Even so we went ahead and

Cobb: sent our boys on up there in 1918, and we had to pay our way into the show like anybody else. We were nothing special. Now it [the 4-H Club Congress] is the most outstanding feature of the International Livestock Show.

But what I'm saying is that General Lee ran into that same trouble. The director of the experiment station, Dr Tracy, was violently opposed to it. With the heavy annual rainfall in Mississippi he just couldn't see any sense in it at all. And he did all he could to hamper Professor McKay. He just couldn't see that irrigation idea at all He said it was just plain nonsense. I think it was the next year that General Lee fired him. Because he never could bring himself to see any value in it at all And it brought about ill feeling between him and other research people on the campus, particularly Professor McKay. Inasmuch as Professor McKay had done what General Lee told him to do, he said, "You go ahead and finish up this program, you go right on through with it, and just forget that Dr Tracy is on the campus." Dr. Tracy had opposed him and he was the man that McKay had to report to. He told him to just forget it, and Dr. Tracy was put out, because he just couldn't see it.

Baum: It is hard to see the necessity for irrigation in a place where there is a lot of rain, but not at the time when you

Baum: need it

Cobb: There is a lot of rain. But he had been on the plantation down there, and he had seen these periods of drought--and you have them at some time every year--that may absolutely ruin a cotton crop; certainly it entirely prevents you from producing vegetables. You just can't do it because they're short-lived to begin with If you haven't got water available now, when you need it, you simply do not have vegetables. Dr. Giles, the president of the college, [Mississippi State University] said to me just a few days ago, in a letter, "Nobody would enter the truck growing business in the state of Mississippi that didn't have auxiliary water available today " How times have changed! And they are growing two bales of cotton to the acre there in the Mississippi delta, up to three, and they occasionally get four Water is the difference.

Baum: They're competing with California cotton now. And they must have irrigation to do it successfully.

Cobb: Well, you have an advantage that they do not have They have the disadvantage of having rain too

APPENDIX

September 7, 1962

Mr. David E. Conrad
Box #8
Southwest Texas State College
San Marcos, Texas

My dear Mr.Conrad:

Thank you for your letter indicating that your history study of the A.A.A. program will be available a little later. I shall be most pleased to have a copy of it when it is available. And while I am making reply, and before I have read your study, I will fulfill a promise I long ago made to myself to set out some rather extraordinary details of the A.A.A. program in black and white for my scrapbook.

Whether I agree with your conclusions or not is beside the point and will in nowise make it less desirable to have it. In your case, knowing that in all probability you are going to be in a profoundly important position of leadership for years to come, your conclusions reflecting your point of view, as they will, are going to be of extraordinary importance.

If I were now doing the same job I was doing in the 1930's and were now confronted with the same circumstances as I was confronted with then, I, no doubt, would do just about what I did in the 1930's. As a basis for all planning and action, looking to making agriculture a paying business, I tried to hold to the basic economic and social facts as they were then. That is what I would do now. And my purpose would be the same. However, there are now relatively few tenants and far fewer farmers as compared to the number of tenants and farms back in the 30's. At that time, we had just come through a depression that not only aggravated a problem that had already become acute but that left both tenants and landowners in such desperate circumstances that it is difficult to see how the situationccould have been much worse. However, neither my basic sociological philosophy nor my basic economic philosophy, or views have changed and certainly my religious beliefs and my spiritual attitude are the same. The foregoing beliefs form the framework for my political belief which can best be summed up in a single phrase: "the American way-of-life." There are just not enough superlatives to tell anybody how profoundly grateful I am for the "American way-of-life." So, were I doing the same job now I was doing in the 30's, I would follow the same general pattern and procedure. Of course, I would use the results of current research and would apply modern methods to help in every way possible

to underpin the program and make it more productive.

Writing history is one thing p making it is another. When you make history you are awfully close to the details.

For instance:

In the announcement attached to your letter, mention is made of the Southern Tenant Farmers Union in the Mississippi Delta - really the delta in Arkansas. This organization is a detail in the history of that period. I was mighty close to it. In connection with it there is the occasion when an Arkansas Negro tenant or laborer had been "murdered." His funeral was preached by a white preacher. Of course, this was in big headlines from coast to coast. A little later, this "dead" Negro was found alive in Chicago. That was not in the papers. I believe this was soon after or just before Norman Thomas was in Arkansas for one of his visits. The Southern Tenant Farmers Union could give you the details. It is a story that is very revealing and helps to emphasize the complexity of our problem and the vexing administrative difficulties that confronted us daily.

A key phrase in your announcement is the statement that "within the AAA, a group of young liberals, especially in the Legal Division, fought to insure greater justice for the tenants but without success." An important detail at this point is the fact that among the more dominant of these young liberals were Alger Hiss, Jerome Frank, Lee Pressman and John Abt. I do not believe that any one of these four men ever lived in the South and not a one of them knew anything at all about agriculture. Even so, they were my attorneys. You know about Mr. Hiss and your researches have told you about the others. Mr. Pressman, I believe, acknowledged that he was a Communist. Jerome Frank got out or was moved out. At last accounts, John Abt was with Americans for Democratic Action. While to the fellow travelers and their leaders the tenant problem was a very convenient tool, as distress of any kind would have been, yet the tenant problem itself was merely incidental to a very elaborate plan to socialize if not communize the Cotton Belt. "Without success" - was the answer to that. However, as the personalities involved, and their supporting cast, so abundantly indicates, defeat was by no means easy.

Still another detail to which I was mighty close, and which had widespread influence, was the organization known as the Southern Conference for Human Welfare. This organization is on the Attorney General's list of subversive organizations. It was organized in Birmingham, Alabama. Mrs. Roosevelt was there to add her influence and help in any way she could. The leadership of this organization, highly skilled in the art of disruption, as well as its members, were very active throughout the entire South and far more adroitly so than the Southern Tenant Farmers Union.

And then there was the National Negro Congress, at the time headed up by one John P. Davis. J. Edgar Hoover says this is one of the organizations that was created or captured by the Communists. The president of that organization, John P. Davis, or his associates, organized the picketing of the Southern Division while I was in Washington. John P. Davis himself appeared at the hearing in my division

developed in that hearing:

We had a hearing unit in our division there in Washington. This unit was organized to meet persons having complaints and in an orderly way try to find out the troubles and then to find satisfactory solutions. One of the few cases that I had the privilege of hearing myself was that involving a Negro woman farmer from near Florence, Alabama. She was brought to Washington and then to my office by the leader of the National Negro Congress who had arranged a hearing for her and who acted as her attorney at the hearing. We took it that he, or his associates, also arranged for the pickets who walked up and down the sidewalks outside our offices carrying placards denouncing the Southern Division for being "unfair" to tenants. All this suggested that her case suited the purpose of the troublemakers better than any other they had found. As a first step in a new publicity drive, she was to be exhibited and publicized as a typical example of the grave injustice being visited upon tenants generally. Certainly it was a case deserving my personal attention. This woman had lived on a farm near Florence, Alabama for many years; had raised her family there and had done well. She had reached the point where she was able to lease the land she farmed and operate it with her own resources as an independent farmer. Under the contract as lessee, which was her status, she was treated in the contract as if she were an independent owner and not as a tenant. The contract she signed and carried out was between her and the federal government and not as between the federal government and the owner of the land she farmed. Under this contract, she was treated exactly as if she had owned the land she farmed. Consequently, all settlements were based upon a contract with her which covered her own independent operations and were made with her personally. With the contract before us, she acknowledged that she had received everything to which she was entitled, as the completed contract showed, just as would have been the case had she been the outright owner of the land she farmed. Some of her troublemaker "friends," however, had gotten hold of her and had convinced her that she was being grossly mistreated by the owner of the land she was farming. This led to a bitter controversy with the owner of the land. The upshot was that she was asked to leave the property at the expiration of her lease. Faced with the probability that she would not be able to find another place, she, of course, was most reluctant to move. We tried to bring about a reconciliation. But as I recall, the controversy had reached a point where there was no other way out but for her to leave. After the facts were all in, it turned out that losing her lease was her real problem and that what she wanted was to have the federal government force its renewal. This case was not unique. Vicious meddling had the same result in thousands of others.

Beyond these cases-in-point, there was the Southern Negro Youth Congress which enjoyed Mrs. Roosevelt's blessing and support and many others including the Communist cell in the United States Department of Agriculture.

Drive after drive was made on me personally, as well as other key members of my Washington organization. The purpose of these drives was to force us out of the government. In one instance, an elaborate attempt was made to lay the groundwork for criminal

prosecution. I was the immediate target. Bill Camp was next. Even so, when all the field work, beginning with an expensive allowance costing thousands of dollars, was completed and the reports were all in and without requiring any testimony on my part, the blanket verdict of the Solicitor General of the U.S. Department of Agriculture was "Mr. Cobb - - has shown due diligence in the performance of duty." A little extra activity involving whisky and women got the leader of one of the investigating teams on this case in trouble. What became of him I do not remember. I do remember, however, that I had fired him for incompetency. and I also remember that he was going to "put me and Bill Camp in jail"!

Now the trouble then with me and the balance of the leadership in my division, which included three very able Negroes, was, as "cell" members and their fellow traveling associates saw it, we were simply too dumb to see the glorious promise there was in it for us all if we would at least become good fellow travelers. And besides that, we were stubborn, contentious, uncooperative and always in the way. So were our wives. The wife of the chief economist of the Department of Agriculture wanted Mrs. Cobb to help her picket the White House. Mrs. Cobb promptly told her to go jump in the Potomac!

If you had asked for it I could have given you the foregoing and much else when you began your study. However, I could not volunteer such information without having younfeel that I was deliberately trying to influence your conclusions. Above all, I would want your conclusions to be your own.

Moreover, I knew that if you did a thorough job of research you would run across these cases as well as countless others yourself and that having found them for yourself you would feel free to complete the details in your own way and to use them in your manuscript in that manner that would give it the balance necessary to remove any semblance of slant as is required in a work of this kind if it is to have trustworthy historic value.

As I look back from this point of hindsight thirty years later, the marvel is that, under the circumstances, we were able to get anything of a constructive character done at all. However, these human interest stories indicate how great our problem was and point up the fact of the countless enemies of our program and of our American way-of-life. Some of these enemies were most vicious, and some naive and foolish. However, they did all they could to create hatred and strife. Feeling that the situation here in the South, very distressing in some areas, was just about perfect for their purpose, they picked the South as a good place to make a grand showing. In this connection, as J. Edgar Hoover keeps saying, it is important to point out the fact these enemies, these "Masters of Deceit," haven't gone away yet.

So to know the history of Agriculture in the Cotton Belt in the 30's, the public must have all the basic facts about the [illegible]

could be no way to evaluate the A.A.A. program as it related to tenants, sharecroppers or anybody else.

Moreover, these cases-in-point tell a lot, of course, that is not found in public print, yet they help confirm the statement I made at the beginning that "when you are making history you are mighty close to the details." It is one thing to have your horse shot from under and another to have somebody tell about it who wasn't in the saddle.

Looking forward with great interest to the receipt of your thesis, I am

Sincerely yours,

CAC:MM

C. A. Cobb, President
Ruralist Press, Inc.

could be no way to evaluate the A.A.A. program as it related to tenants, sharecroppers or anybody else.

Moreover, these cases-in-point tell a lot, of course, that is not found in public print, yet they help confirm the statement I made at the beginning that "when you are making history you are mighty close to the details." It is one thing to have your horse shot from under and another to have somebody tell about it who wasn't in the saddle.

Looking forward with great interest to the receipt of your thesis, I am

Sincerely yours,

C. A. Cobb, President
Ruralist Press, Inc.

CAC:[illegible]

For Mr. Conrad:

As promised in my reply of September 29 to your letter, I am following up with a fairly detailed discussion of subject matter that would have to be covered in a reply to your request for information about the operations of the AAA - 1933 through 1935.

To understand the operations of the Cotton program of the AAA, you have to go back to its beginning in the spring of 1933. It was at that time that I was called to Washington to take over the operations of the Cotton program. I was in Washington until the fall of 1937.

I, of course, do not know how familiar you are with the South or what your research efforts have revealed. However, I am sending you a copy of "Cotton Under the Agriculture Adjustment Act" by Henry I. Richards. This volume was sponsored by and published by the Brookings Institute. And as indicated, it was a study of the Cotton program and was conducted under the direction of Dr. John D. Black of Harvard University and Joseph S. Davis of the Food Research Institute who was also the Director of the Institute of Economics. The facts of the authorship of this study are covered in a statement by Dr. Edwin G. Nourse, Director of Brookings Institute, as shown on Page 5 of the volume. This study was made at my request. The entire files of the Cotton Division were opened to Mr. Richards. He was supplied with copies of all literature, copies of all forms relating to and covering contracts, all correspondence, and with any special information that he deemed necessary to complete an objective study.

At the beginning (1933), I was aware of the extraordinary character of the undertaking involved and consequently wished an authoritative study to be made by a responsible and accepted outside authority. On Page 104 of "Cotton Under the Agriculture Adjustment Act," you will find a summary statement, which statement was extremely gratifying to me in the light of the magnitude of the problems involved, and the difficulty in getting anything approaching effective answers to them. Along with normal difficulties there was the incredible interference which began in Washington with the left-wing activities of Mrs. Roosevelt and her fellow-traveler and communist friends and extended from one end of the Cotton Belt to the other through the activities of various and sundry left-wing groups. The surprising fact is that we were able to get anything of a constructive character done at all. But be all that as it may, the Richards' study rather fully answers many of the questions you have asked.

In devising the program from its beginning, we had the concentrated effort of the ablest agricultural economists in the South, the cooperation of the most sympathetic and far-sighted farmers, together with the full and active assistance of the leadership in the Extension services and agricultural colleges of the several states. The greatest strength of the organization lay in the fine type of individual leadership in the counties responsible for the operation of the program. In the hands of this local leadership, consisting of the white and colored

committeemen were selected by the farmers themselves, the program was operated on the ground by highly trained and experienced leaders and responsible neighbors and not at arm's length by "professionals."

While the program was revolutionary in character and consequently new, yet it was not too difficult to understand or to apply. As Mr. Richards points out in the volume I am sending you, the 1933 cotton crop had already come to harvest when the program got under way. That means that the program at the outset was very much in the nature of a "crash" program. Even so, the study I am handing you, indicates that it was effective in spite of all difficulties.

From the beginning, the most severe criticism of the program came from outside sources - that is, from sources not engaged in farming. And also from the beginning, there were communist-front agitators in the field using every opportunity to stir up dissension and make trouble for everybody.

However, every effort was made at the outset to design the program so that it would represent complete fairness as between all types of tenants and all types of landowners. The overall operation of the program would indicate that fairness as between all groups was largely achieved. We went to extreme lengths to see to it that fairness was the rule and not the exception. There were complaints of unfairness - some were valid - most were not. Most of the complaints that were valid did not arise out of dishonesty but because of misunderstanding or ignorance. There were complaints from individuals in all groups but on the whole there were remarkably few. Most complaints came from regions where deliberate and continuous effort was made for the most part by communist-front and other agitators who had been organized for the purpose of stirring up trouble.

We organized a hearing unit in our division in Washington. This unit was organized to meet persons having complaints and in an orderly way, find out their trouble and seek to find a satisfactory solution. One of the few cases that I had the privilege of hearing myself was that involving a negro woman farmer from near Florence, Alabama. She was brought to Washington and then to my office by the leader of the National Negro Congress who had arranged a hearing for her and who acted as her attorney at the hearing. We took it that he also arranged for the pickets who were walking up and down the sidewalks outside our offices carrying placards denouncing the Southern Division for being "unfair" to tenants. All this suggested that her case suited the purpose of the troublemakers better than any other they had found. She was to be exhibited and publicized as a typical example of the grave injustice being visited upon tenants generally. Certainly it was a case deserving my personal attention. This woman had lived on a farm near Florence, Alabama, for many years, had raised her family there and had done well. She had reached the point where she was able to lease the land [illegible] her own resources as an independent

was treated as an independent owner and not as a tenant. The contract she signed and carried out was between her and the federal government and not as between the federal government and the owner of the land she farmed. Under this contract, she was treated exactly as if she had owned the land she farmed. Consequently, all settlements were based upon a contract with her which covered her own independent operations and were made with her personally. With the contract before us, she acknowledged that she had received everything to which she was entitled as the completed contract showed just as would have been the case had she been the outright owner of the property she farmed. Some of her troublemaker "friends," however, had gotten hold of her and convinced her that she was being grossly mistreated by the owner of the land she was farming. This led to a bitter controversy with the owner of the land. The upshot was that she was asked to leave the property at the expiration of her lease which she was most reluctant to do and which, of course, was most unfortunate. Whether she finally left the property or not, I do not know but apparently the controversy had reached a point where there was no other way out. It turned out that losing her lease was her real problem and she wanted the government to force its renewal and that the contract and settlement under it were quite regular, leaving nothing to complain about.

Many complaints were of this or similar character but few quite as tragic. Knowing that it would probably be difficult for her to find a new place, we in the Washington office sympathized with this woman deeply, but under the circumstances, the best we could do was to suggest to her that she go back home and see her county agents, county committeemen and colored neighbors and see if a reconciliation could not be worked out. One point in this case that cannot be overemphasized - tenants who leased land were treated as farm owners and the contracts they signed gave them the status of farm owners and the right to be treated exactly as if they owned the land they farmed outright.

In your research efforts you probably ran across documents showing that in order to avoid wholesale displacement of tenants and consequent hardship, farmers were required to keep the same number of tenants under the new program as under the old program. It is obvious that this provision was not based on cold economics but upon humanitarian considerations. However, farmers were not required to keep the same identical tenants under the new program because that would have denied the right of contract and would have been clearly illegal. A member of the left-wing group in Washington actually attempted to put a clause in the contract that would force farmers not only to keep the same number of tenants but to keep the same identical tenants. The fact is, however, that every effort was made to see to it that tenants shared according to their rights in whatever progress was made under the program and so far as my information and belief goes, they were quite as enthusiastic about it as anybody else.

of several very able permanent colored employees whom I brought into the southern division of the AAA, which division, of course, developed and administered the program. From the beginning and in order that colored tenants might understand the program and give it their support, these colored leaders helped devise a program of intensive field education to be carried out through the leadership particularly of the colored agricultural colleges and the Baptist and Methodist denominations. This was in addition to the continuous efforts of white and colored extension workers and committeemen and went all the way down from regional and state leaders to local ministers. I do not believe there was a colored pulput in the Cotton Belt (except for a few in the big towns) from which the program was not explained to groups called together for that particular purpose. These meetings followed conferences with church leaders participated in either by myself or other individuals representing the southern division, including our colored employees who were busy throughout the Cotton Belt all the time. To their everlasting credit, our colored leaders were not only quick to see the spiritual and economic values involved but rendered invaluable assistance in helping with the detailed operations of the program. Actually more effort was made to educate tenants than anybody else because those of us in charge of the program understood the program fully and to know what would be expected of them and what they would get out of it.

Again, it should be pointed out that communist-front organizations and other groups of agitators went into action everywhere when the program was announced. Among these were the Southern Conference for Human Welfare, organized in Birmingham, which Mrs. Roosevelt blessed with her presence; the Southern Tenant-Farm Union; and the National Negro Congress. These were the groups that gave us the most trouble and were no doubt the groups that were working most closely with subversives in Washington and elsewhere. Both the Southern Conference for Human Welfare and the National Negro Congress are on the Attorney General's list of communist fronts.

As to violation of contracts, I do not know of a tenant that got into serious trouble but some landlords did and were prosecuted. The records in Washington will reveal who they were. I would not attempt to remember.

At the beginning of the program in the Spring of 1933, about all the tenants and landlords had to divide here in the Cotton Belt was poverty. By the Fall of that year, the situation had greatly improved as the Richards' study indicates. However, for a long period of time, agriculture had been undergoing increasing technological change. This change has moved with great speed as the years have passed. For a long time, the small farmer as well as the traditional tenant farmer had been on the way out for the simple reason that the setup of which they were a part would at best provide little more than a subsistence standard of living. During the past two decades, through combining small farms into larger farms, there has been vast improvement in our

beginning to be of sufficient size, and with sufficient investment of capital, to permit economic operation when in the hands of skillful and businesslike owners. This is a necessary step to profit, better living and stability.

With reference to the "purge," I was, of course, in Washington at the time. The "purge" was not a voluntary action on the part of the Department of Agriculture. The fact is it was carried out with the greatest reluctance. I personally knew each member of the group that was dismissed. For the most part they had been my lawyers and "economists." Mr. Hiss was not let out at the time of the major purge for the simple reason that he was more clever at covering up than were the other members of his group there in the Department of Agriculture. I knew what he was and what the others were but as the Hiss trial indicated, what I knew was difficult to prove. I not only did not intercede for Mr. Hiss but would have been glad to have been rid of him at the beginning. He would have given me much more trouble than he did if he had known anything about agriculture. In this fact I was most fortunate. The whole group that was dismissed would have given us a great deal more trouble than they did had they known anything about agriculture and had not the senators and congressmen from the Cotton Belt looked to those of us from the Cotton Belt itself for leadership and had we not been able at the very outset to prevent the complete take-over of the administration of the program (as was attempted) by the "social planners" and the fellow-travelers there in the Washington office. Fortunately, we were able to keep the work decentralized and in the hands of the Extension forces and resident committeemen of the several states. This not only kept the program close to the people but it kept it in the hands of one of the most intelligent, most responsible and most efficient groups of leaders ever put together. The well-established fact is that county agents, white and colored, and home agents, white and colored, together with state and regional top officials, joined with unstinted effort in putting the program into effect and carrying out its provisions. The program could not have succeeded otherwise.

As to the Myers report: I never knew what Mrs. Myers' job was. She knew nothing about agriculture. It was said she was from Chicago. I always felt that she belonged to the communist cell there in the Department of Agriculture. However that may be, she came to my office one day and told me she was going to Arkansas to make a study of the operation of the program in that area and asked for instructions. I told her that in the first place I was not sending her to Arkansas and consequently had no instructions for her. I did tell her that if she was going to Arkansas for the purpose stated that common courtesy demanded that she report to state authorities telling them her business and asking for their cooperation. I think she went to Memphis. The fact is I do not know where she went or what she went for or whom she saw. If she made a report I never saw it. However her hostile attitude would suggest that she worked with the professional agitators who were quite busy stirring up trouble in that area at that time, some with cells in Arkansas and some with cells

These agitators made a lot of trouble for us and were the source of much unfavorable publicity. For instance, there was a rather lurid story in the papers about an Arkansas Negro tenant who had been murdered and whose funeral was preached by a white Protestant minister. Later this Negro showed up quite healthy and vigorous in Chicago. At the last account, he was still quite alive. In the meantime, the preacher that preached his funeral has been thrown out of the church.

Mrs. Roosevelt's left-wing activities gave us about as much trouble as anything else though she was finally pretty well sized up. For instance, at a meeting called by the Negroes in the Black Belt of Alabama, a resolution was passed inviting her to stay out of the state and pledging continued and unqualified support of the AAA program. I do not believe Mrs. Roosevelt has been back in the state since.

What I have been saying does not mean that a principal product of human nature is always sunshine and roses or sweetness and light. The folks who live in the Cotton Belt are human beings and when you work with a complete cross-section of the people of any area, you, of course, find all sorts of people and all sorts of attitudes - some good - and some bad - and some attitudes are good and some are bad. But on the whole, and in spite of the ever-present troublemakers, all groups showed a gratifying willingness to do the right thing as they understood it.

In the facts I have given you, I think it is quite clear that the tenant has not been the forgotten man. As a matter of fact, we, at all times in the operation of the Cotton program, were more constantly conscious of him, his situation, his needs, than anybody else. The provisions of the program itself bear this statement out. And the manner in which the program was applied everywhere certainly tells the story of continuous and conscientious effort to see that fairness was done. But as you look back at the past, you will realize that in the past the situation of the tenant and the position of the landlord were impossible from the standpoint of genuine social and economic progress.

I hope what I have given you will be helpful in getting a fairly clear picture and a reasonably accurate understanding of the operation of that part of the AAA over which I presided in 1933 and the years which immediately followed. And certainly what I have given you will help you to an objective study - this should be particularly true in the findings of the Brookings Institute.

In the foregoing my discussion has related largely to the operations of the Agricultural Adjustment Administration, and more particularly to some of the details covering the part I played personally in applying the provisions of the AAA to agriculture in the South.

As I look at the title of your study it seems to indicate

have been the objects of gross mistreatment. I think what I have said and the facts presented would indicate that our leaders have been fully conscious of the position of tenants and sharecroppers and have made conscious and successful effort over a long period of time to help them to attain a better status generally. However that may be, it is my feeling that if you are really going to make a thorough and completely objective study that you will have to go much further back than the beginnings of the AAA. As a matter of fact, you will at least have to go back to the period of the Civil War for your starting point and at that point begin your study of the history of the Cotton Belt.

The war left the South prostrate, as you know. Not only that, but up to the recent past it was burdened with all sorts of unfavorable and oppressive legislation. I have particular reference to rail rates, tariff rates, etc. which favored New England and created an economic situation here in the South that forced its people to buy "high" and sell "low." That situation rather fully prevailed up to the first World War and partially for a period since then. As a matter of fact, World War I gave the South its first real opportunity to get its hands on any real money. This really marked a new era. It was the beginning of the South's economic independence. And it was about that same time that the provisions of legislation, some enacted before the turn of the century, looking toward improvement of agriculture, really became effective.

In 1862, the Morrill Land Grant College Act made provision for your state colleges of agriculture for white and Negroes. Some of our best historians say the enactment of this law and the establishment of these colleges marked the greatest single step forward ever made in the history of education. However, it was not until after the turn of the century that these colleges really got underway. In the meantime, Congress has given us the Hatch Act setting up experiment stations. Then in 1914, the Smith-Lever Act setting up agriculture extension work became a law. In 1916, Congress gave us the Smith-Hughes Act providing for vocational education. And in that same year, Congress gave us the Farm Loan Act. In the meantime, much other legislation designed to help rural people to attain a better life has gone on the books. To sum up what is on the books now just about touches every phase of farm life.

If you will go back and study the legislative history of these acts, you will find that a primary purpose back of each one of those acts was to make it possible for all who lived on the land to live better and for those living on the land who did not own land, to become landowners. In connection with all of these laws with the exception of the Land Grant College Act, the history is very clear and in each case sets out the purpose in great detail.

And I would point out that in the application of all these agricultural laws, you will find that they apply to all alike who lived on the land regardless of color or status. As you study the history of our agriculture, you will find that the

its beginning with the application of the Agricultural Extension Act passed in 1914. This act provided for our state extension forces made up of county agents and home agents and their state and national leaders. These forces through direct contact made the findings of experiment stations and research workers in home economics and health available to all farm people alike. With this leadership in the field, farm operations were soon radically improved. In this connection I have only to cite the use of better fertilizer, better seed, better implements, better production methods, better preparation of farm products for market, the better sale of farm products and the improvement and better care of all types livestock together with better homemaking. In the meantime, we have seen the boll weevil brought under control along with the control of many other pests and the most complete elimination of the cattle tick, hog cholera and tuberculosis in livestock. And with it all, farm families were continuously better fed, better clothed, better housed. Also on the human side, we have seen the prevention of hookworm, malaria, typhoid, diptheria, small pox, veneral disease and countless other maladies become a blessed reality. All the people living on the land have shared and shared alike in this progress.

It is worth pointing out that in recent years, again on the human side, we have seen our greatest improvement take place in the education of our farm boys and girls and on the economic side, the revolution in technological progress in the production of crops. All this has applied alike to all persons who live on the land.

Under the application of the Farm Loan Act which dates back to about 1916 and which made money available to farmers through loans for the purchase of land at reasonable rates and payable over a long period of time, farm ownership has increased enormously. This is also true of white and colored farmers alike,as the records will show. As a matter of fact, nowhere else in the world has any nation done so much to promote the economic, social and spiritual well-being of the people who live on the land as has the United States of America. And as pointed out, the legislative history of every act, making progress more easily possible, sets out very clearly that the tenant, whatever the category, has been much in the mind of our leadership. Moreover, most of the leadership responsible for the legislation I have mentioned came from the South. As a consequence they knew the problems of the people of the South at first hand and were able to approach them sympathetically and practically.

In your study, you will, of course, have to keep in mind the facts as they relate to the several types of persons who have made up our farm population here in the South over the last century - sharecroppers, tenants, landowners. You will also have to keep in mind the fact of the economic position of agriculture itself - more particularly that naturally growing out of its relatively low income.

Nothing I have said or intended to convey means that I am not fully aware of the fact that the lot of the tenant has been hard. However, his position of hardship was not a matter of design; it was a natural consequence of the situation already pointed out and that was shared by all. The owner of the land was not spared. Even so, the movement has been forward and upward. And basically when all facts and factors have been brought into the picture and considered, the improvement for all has been vast indeed. And it has been vast indeed largely because of the work of experiment stations and research groups and then the dedication of the leadership of our agricultural forces, particularly as that leadership is represented in county agents and home agents and their associates and co-workers both on the farm and off the farm.

There is a special phase of our general rural progress you will wish to weigh. Of all the youth organizations in the world today, boys' and girls' 4-H Club work stands at the forefront. Beginning in 1910, 4-H Club work has been promoted with increasing effectiveness and without reference to color or status of the farm family from which these children come. And then there is the F.F.A., the organization which has grown out of vocational agriculture. The members of this national organization are meeting in Kansas City at this moment. The members of both of these great youth organizations - 4-H Club work and F.F.A are learning at first hand in their own homes, on their own farms and in their own communities, the truth that "shall make us free."

What I have been saying is by no means an attempt to cover the whole story. It will take your own research and study to do that. From my own point of view, however, it is clear that we have made great progress in meeting our economic and human problems and that greater progress still lies ahead for all who live on the land, regardless of race or category.

I will be tremendously interested in your study when it is completed.

Most sincerely,

C. A. Cobb, President

Henry C. HORNSBY
445 Alta Mesa St.
Riverside, Calif.

Mr. Cully A. Cobb
2632 Fox Hill Drive.
Decatur, Ga.

Dear Mr. Cobb;

I am a Lieutenant Commander in the U. S. Navy working on my Masters Degree at UCLA in my spare time. I plan to write my thesis on the subject The Triple-A and Cotton.

Recently, I had the good fortune of talking with Mr. Chester Davis and Gladys L. Baker of the Historical Research Section of the Dept. of Agriculture. Mrs. Baker gave me your address.

As head of the Cotton Section of the AAA I know that you have a personal knowledge of many things that would add important substance to my paper. In general I would appreciate any material which you might have available in printed form or any material which you might desire to put in a letter. Be assured that I would take good care of it and return as quickly as possible any material which you desired to be returned.

More specifically I would like any material and especially your personal opinion on the following topics.

(1) Those persons who were mainly responsible for formulating the Agricultural Adjustment Act of May 1933; especially any personal interviews which I understand you had with President Roosevelt before and during the writing of the Act.

(2) I am especially interested in your opinion as to whether or not the landlords benefitted more than the tenants. Also your opinion as to whether or not the AAA Cotton Program actually helped the tenant; or did it actually hurt the tenant while the government subsidies actually benefitted mainly the landlords and landowners.

(3) I would appreciate any comments on the Mary Conner Myer report that was never published.

(4) I would further appreciate your opinion as to whether the acreage reduction program was wise or unwise insofar as it caused foreign countries to increase their cotton acreage.

(5) Do you feel that the AAA Cotton Program helped to raise the price of cotton more than, as much as or less than the price rise of items that

the farmer had to purchase? In other words did the AAA Cotton Program actually contribute to increasing the cotton farmer's purchasing power?

I realize that I have ask you some questions, and maybe too many, that will be difficult to answer, but I would sure appreciate your personal opinion on as many as possible. As head of the Cotton Section I feel that your opinions are the most valid and intelligent that I can obtain and will make an invaluable contribution to my Master's Thesis.

Thanking you in advance, I remain

Yours sincerely

Henry C. HORNSBY

July 6, 1965

Mr. Henry C. Hornsby
445 Alta Mesa Street
Riverside, California

My dear Mr. Hornsby:

I have your recent letter with reference to your work toward securing your Masters degree at UCLA and I am happy to help in any way that I can.

Very shortly after being assigned to the job of implementing the Cotton Division of the AAA, I asked the Brookings Institute to assign some one to make a study of the operations of the Cotton Division of the AAA program to which request the Institute very willingly acceded. They assigned Mr. Henry I. Richards to make this study. Mr. Richards worked very closely with the leadership of the several sections of the Cotton Division and, of course, was given access to all records. Mr. Richards submitted his study "Cotton Under the Agricultural Adjustment Act" in 1934. His study covered developments up to July, 1934. Under another cover, I am mailing you a copy of his report which I wish you would return to me at your earliest possible convenience. The whole study is one that will be of tremendous interest to you.

But that discussion covering the effects of the Cotton program will be the most definite answer to one of your questions, which question has reference to the actual value of the program. Or, to put it another way - was the program helpful or not? Mr. Richards' study indicates very definitely that the program was of enormous value in starting the Cotton Belt back on the road to better days. It is Mr. Richards' findings that the program not only helped those farmers who cooperated but helped the non-cooperating farmers and all business as well. You will find this discussion on pages 78, 79, 80, 81 and 82. This discussion will be of great value in answering most of the questions you have asked about the program. Earlier discussions appearing in this volume will, of course, be helpful.

I did have a number of conferences with President Roosevelt before he became President. These discussions had to do with the agricultural situation in the South. How helpful they were I, of course, had no way of knowing. Out of it the President got a better understanding of what the real problem here in the South was. My last discussion with him before he became President was at the Little White House at Warm Springs here in Georgia.

As to your second question, if it could be expressed percentage-wise, I imagine the tenants actually benefited more than the landlords. This also could prove true as the position of the landlords and the tenants was related to future development. The application of the program certainly gave both the landlords and the tenants a new sense of security as well as the actual fact of greater security itself. In the application of the program, everything was done that could be done to see to it that both the tenant and the landlord was protected fully in his own right.

With reference to the Mary Conner Myer incident, I have little information that would be at all helpful. What I do know is that somebody in the Department of Agriculture sent her to Memphis and I think the prupose was to investigate the tenant-landlord relationships in Arkansas. Mrs. Myer came to my office one morning and told me she had been selected to make an investigation in Arkansas and said she would like instructions. I told her that I had not selected her to make an investigation and that I knew nothing of why she had been selected, who selected her and, of course, that I had no instructions. I did tell her, however, that as she was going into Arkansas as a representative of the Department of Agriculture, common courtesy demanded that she make her presence known to the Department workers in Arkansas, namely the Extension workers and those in charge of the Cotton program. As to whatever report she may or may not have made, I have no information whatsoever. I did not see any report and have no first-hand information from anybody that did see it. What Mrs. Myers' basic purpose was I never knew. Whatever it was I can never conceive of it as being very constructive.

As to Point 4 in your list of topics, I do not believe the Cotton program itself had any appreciable effect on cotton production outside the United States either one way or the other. I think every nation that had cotton production potentialities at that time was working to develop these potentialities and I think they have continued to increase cotton production over the years. This would have happened whatever we may or may not have done, or yet may do at any time in this field. It is in the economic interest of every nation to produce food and fibre on its own soil to meet its own needs when this can be done economically.

As to topic 5 in your letter, I think the best answer is in Mr. Richards' study. In the intervening years, and necessarily because of "the program," the South has made phenomenal progress. A case in point will illustrate what I am saying. Back in 1933 when the program was started, I had a conversation with Secretary Wallace in his office, and during that conversation I expressed the belief that if the program as outlined went over with a fair degree of success that it would lay the foundation for progress in cotton production that would soon result in lifting the average acreage yield in 1933 to a bale or more to the acre. In 1933, the yield per acre was 209.4 pounds according to the

Mr. Wallace's reply was "We will not see that in your lifetime nor in mine." The answer to that according to the final 1964 statistical report of the United States Department of Agriculture, C.R.-P-2-1, is that the yield was 517 pounds. This is more than a bale to the acre by a good margin. And Mr. Wallace and I are still alive!

In the meantime, the acreage yield, as noted, has not only come up from less than one-half bale to an acre but is now close to a bale and a quarter. Indeed many farmers are now producing two to three bales or better to the acre and the forecast based on current study of cotton production per acre will be 700 pounds.

Looking back to the beginning of the program, the total value of the 1933 cotton crop of 13,177,000 bales stood at $604,000,000.00, the value of the 1964 crop of 15,180,000 bales was $2,225,846,000.00.

In my discussion with Secretary Wallace, I cited the records of the 4-H Club members from one end of the Cotton Belt to the other. These records based on carefully checked production records ranged anywhere from a bale to more than two bales per acre. It was my expressed feeling then that if 4-H Club boys could produce like that, there was no good reason why all cotton producers could not raise the average production per acre to a bale or more throughout the Cotton Belt. As indicated, in the meantime we have seen this prediction fulfilled with quite a bit on the plus side. And increased production per acre can be expected to move on up in the years ahead.

We have seen comparable increase in production of all other crops and in all types of livestock. The fundamental reason lies in basic education in agriculture and particularly, in the economics and techniques involved. This practical training had much of its beginning in 4-H Club work. These boys made practical application of the findings of experiment stations and of all our laboratories. When these boys took over farming as adults, they knew what they could do and how to do it. We today have the best educated farmers in the world. Many of them are college graduates and top-flight scientists. Their success as farmers is undisputed testimony to this fact.

As to the future of the farm program, you will note that Mr. Richards expressed a good many doubts. I harbored many doubts myself before I left Washington.

In the summer of 1937 in an address at a statewide meeting of farmers in Little Rock, Arkansas, I made a statement with reference to what the future held for the farm program in which you may be interested. My statement was to the effect that "in the very nature of the program itself are found the seeds of its own destruction." Continuous operation of the program foreshadows the concentration of vast authority in an all-wise and all-powerful politically dominated bureaucracy in Washington." I followed that with this language. "As director of my division of

jury; inherent in this combination is the power of life and death. This is not good." I stated further that by the very nature of the facts of life as they related to governmentally operated farm programs, or programs of any other type, that those in authority had no chance but to follow every dollar to its final use and account for it and that out of that responsibility, would arise rules and regulations without end. And that the inevitable result would be complete control from Washington of every step from planting to harvest and sale. The answer as I saw it would be a bureaucracy of incalculable dimensions. I reminded them again that no man living, or in my judgement, would ever live who would be wise enough to handle such power as I had over the cotton industry in a manner that would translate it into freedom of movement, freedom of decision and freedom of action by those in the industry. I cited the fact that Solomon tried it and was the last king that Israel ever had. It should be pointed out here that at the time the authorities in Washington knew I was going to resign in the coming fall.

And now nearly thirty years later we find much of that prediction coming true. The truth is a very serious agricultural situation confronts us. And it is tragically evident that the vast bureaucracy in Washington does not have the answer.

Going back to 1933, it was not thought at that time that the program would be permanent. It was inaugurated to bring an end to the current tragic situation if possible. However, like the emergency or nuisance taxes and other temporary measures that were placed upon the statute books at that time, it is still with us. Let's hope the removal of some of the nuisance taxes is a good omen.

Very truly yours,

C. A. Cobb, President
Ruralist Press, Inc.

CAC:MM

December 10, 1965

Mr. Henry C. Hornsby
890 Plum Street
Riverside, California

My dear Mr. Hornsby:

I have your recent letter with further reference to the AAA Cotton Program. In my first letter to you I should have done what I am going to do now in order to help you construct a better background.

The morning I arrived in Washington to head up the Cotton Program, I was met at the depot by an Associated Press reporter. After introducing himself, he remarked that he had been informed that I would head up the Cotton Program and that he would like a statement. What he really wanted to know was what my approach would be. I told him that my job as I saw it would be "to help make farming a paying business in the Cotton Belt." It was clear, however, that this answer was a little too prosaic and not at all what he had expected. He then rather sharply asked who had recommended me, who appointed me, etc. I told him that I was in Washington at the invitation of Secretary Wallace. I realized later that he had expected me to indicate that I was in Washington to inaugurate a vast and sweeping program of social reform in the Cotton Belt. I also found later that he really had good reason to believe that I was there for that purpose for I very promptly discovered that a program replete with all the fancy social trimmings had been agreed upon and that I would be expected to pick it up and go from there.

Though completely past understanding, the grand new design would by-pass colleges of agriculture, Extension work, and all the other long established agricultural forces in the field. And quite as incredible, all state and all local governments were to be completely ignored, with everything centered in and responsible to Washington. However, much to the dismay of the master planners, many of whom knew little about agriculture and still less about the South and its cotton problem, the obviously impossible grand design was rejected outright. As enumerated above, the forces then in the field were drafted. They were drafted by decree and by no less a personage than President Roosevelt himself. In this decision is found the real answer to the amazing achievements of the next few months.

Let me quote here from Page 48 of a historic booklet by J. A. Evans, "Recollections of Extension Work." This quotation will shed a lot of light on what I have just said.

"Cobb was firmly convinced that the use of the Extension Service was absolutely necessary to the success of any adjustment

plan. He decided that the thing to do was to call a conference of the Southern Extension Directors at once to tell them what the A.A.A. was considering ***. He asked the Secretary for permission to call such a meeting. The Secretary set a conference of the A.A.A. people for eight o'clock the same night to decide whether or not Mr. Cobb's request should be granted. This was the show-down as to what course was to be pursued regarding the use of the Extension Service. I was the only Extension person present at this conference. I was there because Mr. Cobb asked me to come and because, in fact, he was at that time expecting me to be his assistant. The Secretary, M.C. Wilson, Tugwell, Brand, Ezekiel and others of the A.A.A. staff so far selected, in all ten or twelve people, were present. It was midnight before Mr. Cobb could get definite permission to call the conference of Extension Directors. The Secretary did not talk but several others were on record against the proposal to use the Extension Service. Numerous objections were urged and the question was asked "What will we say to Senator Murphy (Iowa) and these other senators and congressmen who say they don't want anything to do with the Extension Service?"

An Incident.

"I feel sure that the Secretary and Mr. Wilson wanted to use the Extension Service and indeed felt that it was necessary to do so but Ezekiel, Tugwell, Brand and others wanted to form a separate organization or at least talked that way.

"An incident will illustrate the situation. The Secretary sat in the middle of the room with Brand on one side of him and I think either Wilson or Ezekiel on the other. The rest of us ranged around the wall facing them. Both Cobb and myself made every argument we could in support of the proposition that the use of the Extension Service was necessary to the success of any plan adopted. At the close of one of Mr. Cobb's remarks in which he had spoken of the Extension Directors and the confidence farmers in the states had in the Extension organizations, Tugwell, who was sitting in the line with us got up to go, remarking, "Well, you fellows have a lot more confidence in these Extension Directors than I have." As he walked behind the Secretary's chair, the Secretary looking back over his shoulder, smilingly said to him, "You don't seem to have much confidence in the Extension Directors," and Tugwell, leaning down and in a lower voice, replied, "I haven't a damned bit of confidence in any of them." But in the end Mr. Cobb prevailed and permission to take the steps requested by him was given. I have always felt that by his determined stand for the use of the Extension Service, Mr. Cobb did both the Colleges and the A.A.A. a very great service."

It will also shed a lot of light to add the following names to those Mr. Evans lists: Jerome Frank, Lee Pressman, Alger Hiss, John Apt and Beany Baldwin. Of course, this by no means completes the list. However, the public record of these will tell you what you need to know about them personally and what direction their energies and influences would take.

The cotton problem is as old as the South. It had its real beginning with the close of the Civil War. At that time landowners and tenants were all set free to dig what they could out of the ruins. And under the restraint imposed on a subjugated people, they had no alternative but to pull themselves up by their own bootstraps. The fact is the southern states were not able to get their hands on any real money, the one thing necessary to throw off the bondage of colonialism, until World War I destroyed the old pattern. The old pattern was that of a controlled economy providing the raw material for the factories of those who were in control.

Between World War I and the financial crash of 1929, real progress got under way in the Southern states in spite of the devastating ravages of the cotton boll weevil. Beginning with the invasion of the boll weevil, agriculture in the Southern states has undergone an unprecedented revolution. In the early and most destructive days of the boll weevil, I saw sharecroppers and tenants leave the South in trainloads. They went first to St. Louis and then to industrial centers outside the Cotton Belt. This exodus has continued in diminishing numbers down to the present time.

Competition from other fibres, technological progress and continuously rising costs of production forced the adoption of every available means to achieve maximum efficiency in all phases of production and handling. Two things in particular forced the abandonment of the ancient cotton plantation - diversification of crops to restore the fertility of the soil and to end the one-crop system, and vast technological improvements in all phases of crop production.

The result has been a continuously diminishing need for hand labor. For instance, fifty years ago there were millions of mules in the Cotton Belt. Today there are practically none. Fifty years ago, mules supplied the power and sharecroppers and tenants supplied the vast need for hand labor. That need for both has all but disappeared.

Three weeks ago, I saw one man with a one-row cotton picker harvesting cotton at the rate of twenty-five bales in a single day. At a high automated and very modern gin nearby, the sample produced was close to what it would have been had the cotton been picked by hand.

Shortly after my arrival in Washington to head up the Cotton Division in a conference with Secretary Wallace, he asked what we might expect under the program. I told him that if the program went as I believed it would that within a short period of time, we would be harvesting a bale of cotton to the acre. His reply was "Not in your lifetime or mine." In spite of the fact that Mr. Wallace died a few weeks ago yet he lived to see that prediction come true. In 1932, the year before this discussion, the average cotton yield per acre stood at 173 pounds on 36,542,000 acres. The crop of the year stood at 13,000,200 bales. Mr. Wallace could not bring himself to believe that the average yield

could be lifted to a bale to the acre. I told him that my prediction was based on the records of hundreds of 4-H Cotton Club members from one end of the Cotton Belt to the other. Many of these club members produced yields far in excess of a bale per acre. In 1943 on 15,180,000 acres of cotton the average yield was 517 pounds per acre, producing a total crop of 15,180,000 acres of cotton the average yield was 517 pounds per acre, producing a total crop of 15,180,000 bales. In 1965, the average yield per acre was 531 pounds on 13,632,000 acres. The total cotton crop of 1965 was 15,143,498 bales. Mr. Wallace saw these figures for both years.

I do not know about Will Clayton's observation. You will recall, however, that in order to prevent the wholesale release of sharecroppers and tenants, a provision was written into the contract to the effect that landlords would be required to keep the same number of tenants that they had the year before. Whatever view one may wish to take of this provision, under the circumstances, it was convincing evidence of the acceptance of humanitarian responsibility. Landowners recognized it as being just that. Long before, however, it was inevitable that the whole plantation system with its familiar low standard of living and restricted opportunity had to go.

Now about our field organization. If you will read carefully the discussion of Mr. Richards' study, pages 16, 17, 18, 19, 26, 29 and 55, I think you will get a fairly clear idea of how our operating force was put together. I would not know how to put together a more experienced, a more intelligent and a more honorable organization than the one we had. It represented the very best in solid American citizenship.

Mr. Richards' study also gives many details indicating the breadth of the program, the limitations inherent, as well as the widespread social and economic effects that were bound to arise in its application. And we must remember that the program was launched and conducted under the most pressing circumstances.

Much of the difficulty in the field came from outside interference. Those who wished the program to take the direction of vast social reform were disappointed with everything and brought all the pressure they could to change it or defeat it. You will recall that at this time there was a very vigorous communist cell in the Department of Agriculture. Some of its members were in key positions. This cell also had its co-workers in many areas of the Cotton Belt. Under the leadership of local and regional outsiders, they hastily set up organizations. The names of the most powerful are on the Attorney General's list of subversive organizations.

They gave us all the trouble they could. The Southern Conference for Human Welfare (on the list of subversives) was probably the most effective of these groups. With the assistance of Mrs. Roosevelt, this organization was set up in Birmingham. From the beginning it was under the influence of outside leftist

Though it was organized in Arkansas, it gave more trouble in California than in the Cotton Belt. I do not know if it was on the list of subversives or not. The National Negro Congress, a communist-dominated outfit, and a number of leftist youth groups were also among the troublemakers. I forgot to say that Norman Thomas, who was on T.V. the other day, got in his "two bits." You will have to check and measure all unfavorable comment in the light of these facts. The following will serve as a case-in-point.

The only complaint that came to me directly was from a plantation just out of Florence, Alabama. John Davis of the National Negro Congress brought the complainant, a Negro woman, to Washington and demanded a hearing. He was sure he had a perfect example of dishonesty and of cruel and inhuman treatment. The hearing was conducted by the Hearing Unit of the Southern Division before which the woman and her representative, John Davis, appeared. E. A. Miller was in charge of the Hearing Unit. At the time of the hearing, pickets with placards denouncing the Southern Division for unfair treatment of tenants were parading on the sidewalk outside my office. This was the crowning feature of Davis' carefully planned publicity. The papers were full of it, pictures and all. However, the fact that the basis for picketing and the sensational publicity was completely false, there was no way to counteract the damage done. Inasmuch, however, as there is nothing particularly sensational about an honestly completed contract of this kind, the papers and magazines had no further interest in the matter.

When Davis and his client appeared, he demanded to see and examine the contract covering his client's operations. We had no objection. Her file had been completed and closed. However, we listened to Mr. Davis and the story of the woman. We then reviewed the contract. Being a cash tenant, the contract was with the woman herself. As was her right, she had signed as if she were the owner of the land. Her landlord was not a party to the contract. The woman had not only signed the contract personally but had complied with all its provisions and had personally received all payments.

During the hearing the real reason for this woman's visit to Washington came to light. Her landlord had asked her to leave. The real trouble was that she had come under the influence of agitators who had convinced her that she had been denied her rights and otherwise grossly wronged by her landlord. That led to a series of quarrels that so antagonized her landlord that her landlord felt that there was nothing left for her to do but let her go. It developed that this woman had been on the place for many years; that in the meantime she had raised her family, had bought and paid for her own mules, other livestock and farm implements. She admitted that she had operated independently, had never had any trouble before, that she had done well and had been happy. What had happened was, of course, most unfortunate and we told her that when she went back to Florence, we would have the county agent try to bring about a reconciliation, if it were possible. While I do not know, I imagine that was what happened

While, as I stated, the Florence, Alabama was the only case that came to me personally, there were undoubtedly many complaints of similar character. It was our policy to follow up all complaints promptly. Even so, this was the only case I knew about where a tenant was actually asked to leave. In this connection you will note there were four types of contracts. Mr. Richards discusses them on Page 109 of his book.

Now about the sharecroppers. Under the contract they were treated as if they owned the land they farmed. This vested interest treatment is the basis of my statement that on a percentage basis the tenant fared better than anybody else. Moreover this vested interest treatment is another case of a deep sense of humane responsibility.

I am attaching Ralph McGill's column clipped from the Atlanta Constitution of November 28, 1965. In this column Mr. McGill discusses Mr. Wallace. This discussion will be helpful in building your background.

The story of cotton between the years 1932 and 1965 is a story of progress that surely is without parallel in history. It is a veritable revelation of what human ingenuity intelligently applied can do for a people, for a region, and for a nation. And the final chapter has not been written.

Of course, for the full story, it would help to go back to the Civil War, to the coming of the Land Grant colleges and to the establishment of Extension work in 1914. Congressman Lever was from South Carolina and Senator Hoke Smith was from Georgia.

Sorry to have made this statement so long, yet I felt that if I was going to be at all helpful, it should provide the information that I have given you. And I hope you will find it very useful.

Very truly yours,

C. A. Cobb, President
Ruralist Press, Inc.

CAC:MM
Enc.

P.S.: There was some discrepancy in the total figures with reference to the number of bales harvested in 1965 that I have not had time to check with the government. So what I did was to take the number of acres in cultivation and the yield per acre to get the total number of pounds of lint produced. I divided this figure by 478 pounds of lint cotton required to make a bale. The "standard" bale is made up of 478 pounds of lint and twenty-two pounds of bagging and ties.

Added to Mr. Hornsby's letter in Mr. Cobb's handwriting:

The revised indicated yield of the U.S. Department of this date for 1965 is 15,189,000 bales. The 1965 acreage still stands at 13,632,000. The yield is now given as 534 pounds per acre.

Ruralist Press
INCORPORATED
713 Glenn Street S.W. Atlanta, Georgia 30310
Telephone 753-1121

September 23, 1966

Mrs. Willa Baum,
Head, Regional Oral History Office
Bancroft Library
University of California
Berkeley, California

My dear Mrs. Baum:

A few days ago, Mr. W. B. Camp and I were discussing the work you are doing in assembling certain information relative to Mr. Camp's activities down through the years and it seems to us that I might be helpful to you in supplying information that probably otherwise might not come to your attention.

To that end, I am attaching a copy of "Cotton Under the Agricultural Adjustment Act" by Henry I. Richards. Under the direction of Dr. Nourse, whom I knew, Mr. Richards made this study for the Brookings Institute. It was done at my request. Not everybody in the Department of Agriculture was enthusiastic about a study of this character. However, our group in the Cotton Division felt that it would be most helpful - that indeed it was essential that we have the benefit of an objective study and appraisal of the value of our work for guidance in the future. You will find the study valuable.

I am also attaching my own biographic sketch as it appears in a book of biographic sketches of '08 graduates of Mississippi State University. Very recently I supplied a considerable amount of information to a student at Riverside, California who was working on a post-graduate degree. I am enclosing a copy of that.

In my own biographic sketch you will find a quotation from a book by Mr. J. A. Evans. I discussed this briefly as you will note.

At the very beginning of the AAA program, I was asked to come to Washington to take over the cotton division. That was the first division to be set up. I was rather fully acquainted with the cotton problem in the old South but was not too familiar with the problems of cotton in the West, particularly in California. The need, therefore, was very great for someone intimately acquainted with the cotton problems of that territory. Mr. Camp, of course, was the most natural choice. He had gone to California after graduation from Clemson to establish an experient station designed to se[illegible] the
indu[illegible] ourse,
he kn[illegible] West.

to our group an ability that made an immeasurable contribution to the furtherance of our program. I am sure that except for his intimate knowledge of the whole cotton problem and his very great courage and his fine ability to help develop our overall plans and then to apply them that we would have had infinitely more trouble in holding our program within practical bounds than was the case.

Our chief problem was not in the Cotton Belt. It was with the radicals in and out of the Department of Agriculture whose ideological approach to everything was so completely at variance with sound economics and indeed with our entire concept of what was necessary to preserve our American way of life that there was no basis for cooperation.

I am sure that in your discussions with Mr. Camp he has informed you of the day-to-day fight we had with the communist cell and their fellow-travelers in the Department of Agriculture and their "friends" out in the states.

However, some of our difficulties went back to the very beginnings of the land-grant college system and even more importantly to the establishment of extension work. Because of a fundamental difference in approach there was always enmity and jealousy between those directing the colleges of agriculture and extension work in the North and in the South. At the beginning, the land-grant college idea was almost wholly unwelcome by the leadership of education in many states. In many states, extension work was also unwelcome. In those states, extension work was regarded as an action program and consequently outside the activities of a university. Our cotton program was precedent setting. That made it easier for our enemies to enlist outside influences. Many attempts were made during our years in Washington to destroy both Mr. Camp and myself. They, of course, failed. I was asked to fire Mr. Camp. My very prompt answer was "fire me first." Nobody was fired! I am sure Mr. Camp has told you all about this. My biographic sketch I believe will be helpful to a degree on some of these points.

But be all the foregoing as it may, I hope that what I am supplying will be helpful in completing the record of a most marvelous man who has lived a most marvelously successful life.

Most sincerely,

C. A. Cobb

C. A. Cobb, President
Ruralist Press, Inc.

CAC:MM
Enc.

Ruralist Press
INCORPORATED

713 Glenn Street S.W. Atlanta 10, Georgia
Telephone PLAZA 3-1121

March 1, 1968

Mrs. Willa Baum, Head
Regional Oral History Office
University of California
Berkeley, California

My dear Mrs. Baum:

In the months since we had our interview, I have gotten together a good deal of important and very helpful material to document and otherwise improve our whole historic interview. The Underwood and Underwood photographs and the group picture of the Southern Division will add a lot.

Just very recently I found a number of copies of a monthly publication that we used to get out at Mississippi State that went specifically to 4-H Club members. A final copy in 1918 tells the whole story of the first group of 4-H Club boys that visited the International Livestock show at Chicago and whose visit marked the date of the beginning of the present National 4-H Club Congress. I am sending you a photostatic copy of the whole four pages of this publication together with a specially made photograph that gets about all out of the front page cut that could be gotten.

Together with this particular issue I received a number of other copies that tell the story of subsequent years - but this is the information you need to document the statement I made that this group of boys who went from Mississippi and Oklahoma in 1918 to the International Livestock show marked the beginning of the 4-H Club Congress.

Sam Bledsoe has sent me a lot of material quoting the statement that President Roosevelt made about Senator George in his address at Barnesville, Georgia when he made his historic attempt to purge the Senator. Sam gave me permission to say in the oral history that it is he who was able to get the Roosevelt statement direct from the final draft of the speech. When the statement was handed to Senator George at the time of the speech, he was well prepared to take care of himself which he did in a magnificent and devastating manner.

I am also sending a copy of pages 105,106 and 107 of the Spring 1967 issue of the Tennessee Historical Quarterly. This quarterly is published by the Tennessee Historical Society in cooperation with the Tennessee Historical Commission. You will note on page 106, the last two sentences on that page refer to the purge of the radicals. The particular sentence that is probably the most important as documentary material is this: "Cully Cobb, chief of the Cotton Section and native-born [illegible] leader of [illegible] the
liber[illegible].

I have gone over the manuscript carefully and think it is in good shape. As I find other material that would be of documentary importance, I will send it on in.

I am also returning the agreement which I have signed.

You will also find attached copies of photographs that were made of us there on the grounds of the hotel. I think they are good and I believe you will like them. We are still hoping you will come and see us.

Sincerely,

C. A. Cobb

C. A. Cobb, President
Ruralist Press, Inc.

CAC:MM
Enc.

P.S.
The statement about 4-H club work will be found in the Scott interview— I am mailing the manuscript under another cover
C.A.C

Ruralist Press
INCORPORATED
713 Glenn Street S.W. Atlanta 10, G
Telephone PLAZA 3-1121

March 12, 1968

Mrs. Willa Baum, Head
Regional Oral History Office
The Bancroft Library
University of California, Berkeley
Berkeley, California 94720

My dear Mrs. Baum:

I am having color prints made of the picture of you, Mr. Camp and myself and will get them to you at an early date. I will send you about a half dozen so that you will have what would appear to be enough to meet your immediate demand. If you need more, let me know and I will get more later. I imagine it will be a week or ten days before they come. The films have to be sent to Rochester to be processed. If they were black and white, we could get them done here.

Glad you liked the manuscript and particularly what I did to present the facts about Mary Conner Myers' report as I knew them. You may wish to break that story down into questions and answers. You may also wish to break down the story with reference to Senator George into questions and answers. Please feel free to present it in a manner that is best suited for the preparation of your oral history.

You have my permission to send the manuscript on to anyone who can qualify. The requirements for all other institutions will be the same as they are there at Berkeley.

If you need more material, or answers to questions that you need discussion about, please let me know.

Sincerely,

C. A. Cobb, President
Ruralist Press, Inc.

CAC:MM

Ruralist Press
INCORPORATED
713 Glenn Street S.W. Atlanta, Georgia 3031(
Telephone 753-1121

March 13, 1967

Mrs. Willa Baum, Head
Regional Oral History Office
Bancroft Library
University of California
Berkeley, California

My dear Mrs. Baum:

Thank you for your letter, the transcript of the interview and other material.

I am preparing a short discussion of the Conrad book and will get it on to you as early as possible.

I will carefully go over the interview transcript and as suggested, will make such revisions as seem necessary to clarity.

With reference to my resignation in 1937, early in the Spring of that year, I informed Chester Davis that I had done about all I could in Washington and in any event I had acquired controlling interest in the Ruralist Press here in Atlanta - an institution with which I had been associated for a long period of time and that I would return to Atlanta to take over the operations of the Ruralist Press as its president. I told him also that I was telling him at that time so as to obviate the possibility of publicity of the type that might indicate that I had been unceremoniously kicked out, with all sorts of nasty speculation and implications as to the reason why. Such publicity was characteristic of that era. And it related especially to those who had served in a more or less controversial area and had not gone along with the fellow travelers. In departing I was given a dinner by Secretary Wallace and my staff gave me a beautifully inscribed Hamilton watch. There was no unfavorable publicity.

I will make reference to this in the transcription so you will have it as you rework it.

With reference to the agreement, it ought to be available to any student to use in any historic or economic investigation or study. However, I would not want it to be used, or any part of it, for the preparation of books, articles, etc. without permission. It is so easy to take a statement out of context and have it mean exactly the opposite of what it meant in its proper place.

sure I

In both of these cases, the experience has been thrilling and I am glad that what we put down will add new dimensions to your work in this field. I will help complete it with copies of photographs we made there during the filming of the beer commercial.

As indicated, I will be getting comments on the Conrad book to you at an early date.

Most sincerely,

C. A. Cobb

C. A. Cobb, President
Ruralist Press, Inc.

CAC:MM

PARTIAL INDEX

Willa Klug Baum

Grew up in Middle West and Southern California.
B.A , Whittier College, in American history and philosophy, teaching assistant in American history and constitution.
Newspaper reporter
M.A., Mills College, in American history and political science, teaching fellow in humanities.
Graduate work, University of California at Berkeley, 1949-1954, in American and California history; teaching assistant in American history and recent United States history
Adult school teacher, Oakland, in English and Americanization, 1948-1967, author of teaching materials for English
Summer session instructor in English for foreign students, Speech Department, University of California at Berkeley
Interviewer and then head of Regional Oral History Office, 1954 to present, specializing in water and agricultural history.
Council member of national Oral History Association, 1967-1969

CPSIA information can be obtained
at www.ICGtesting.com
Printed in the USA
LVHW081345190220
647490LV00007B/115